THE STUDENT'S GUIDE TO
Writing
Essays

The Student's Guide Series from Kogan Page

The Student's Guide to Passing Exams, Richard Burns
The Student's Guide to Preparing Dissertations and Theses, Brian
  Allison
The Student's Guide to Writing Essays, David Roberts

THE STUDENT'S GUIDE TO
Writing
Essays

DAVID ROBERTS

KOGAN PAGE

First published in 1997
Reprinted 1999

Apart from any fair dealing for the purposes of research or private study, or criticism or review, as permitted under the Copyright, Designs and Patents Act 1988, this publication may only be reproduced, stored or transmitted, in any form or by any means, with the prior permission in writing of the publishers, or in the case of reprographic reproduction in accordance with the terms of licences issued by the Copyright Licensing Agency. Enquiries concerning reproduction outside those terms should be sent to the publishers at the undermentioned address:

Kogan Page Limited
120 Pentonville Road
London N1 9JN

© David Roberts, 1997

British Library Cataloguing in Publication Data

A CIP record for this book is available from the British Library.

ISBN 0 7494 2192 4

Typeset by Kogan Page
Printed and bound in Great Britain by Clays Ltd, St. Ives Plc

Contents

Introduction

Advice about how to write essays is not in short supply. Tutors comment on work, grade it, give tutorials, distribute handouts, set up study groups, take part in e-mail discussions, arrange conferences, and sometimes go to the desperate lengths of writing books on the subject. With so much advice around, what will you find here that you won't get elsewhere?

This guide begins from the simple idea that the language you are expected to produce for academic work is different from the language you use for everyday purposes. In many ways, indeed, it is a foreign language, with all kinds of strange rules that you won't encounter anywhere else. How does anyone manage to learn such a language? The fundamental processes bear little relationship to the pattern of advice most students receive about how to write. To learn another language, you need these three things:

- *exposure*, because if you don't know what the language looks like, you have little chance of reproducing it;
- *graded learning*, because you wouldn't normally attempt, say, a novel in French just after completing a GCSE in it;
- *repetition*, because all language use is, in part, a mechanical exercise which can only become second nature if it is revisited.

Compare this with what often happens on degree-level courses. There may be no exposure, because you won't necessarily get the chance to look at anyone else's work; graded learning may be completely absent, since most students start writing full-blown essays from the outset; the chance to repeat skills is, likewise, often overtaken by the need to move on to the next stage of the curriculum.

In this guide, by contrast, you move through elements of essay writing at a controlled pace, from core skills to subject applications, with plenty of opportunity for practice and reflection. You won't be asked to write an essay before you've learned how to write a paragraph. In the first instance, relatively simple examples of writing are used to get you thinking about principles of structure and

1

organisation, so that you're not bombarded too early with material that is hard to assimilate. In addition, you get exposure to the styles and approaches demanded by three mainstream subjects, so that instead of being confused by conflicting advice from tutors in discrete fields you can work at the conventions which prevail in each.

There is a further significant difference between this guide and others. This is a workbook: it is designed to foster learning through doing, not just through comprehending. As you work through it, you should have a pen and paper to hand so that you can put into practice *straight away* the advice it has to offer. If you don't make the effort to do that, the book will have lost half its value. Approximately 50 hours should be enough for you to make your way through it, assuming that you choose only one of the subject sections. Bear in mind that the work is cumulative, so make sure you can *do* each section before moving on – don't skip ahead because you think you know something already. Trials of this book have indicated that it has at least as much to offer highly competent essay writers as those who struggle to produce anything coherent.

The fact that it is a workbook carries one disadvantage: it can't be nearly as comprehensive in its advice as some other published guides, otherwise it would fill many more pages (and hours of your time) than it should. Its purpose is to give you controlled practice in a variety of key areas, so providing a strong foundation for future work. Above all, it aims to show you how to make use of your greatest learning resource in improving your writing – your own reading. By giving you directed work on appropriate texts, this guide pursues a paradoxical finding witnessed by the experience of countless tutors, not to mention research projects and ancient rhetorical treatises: that learning to write well is partly a function of reading widely and intelligently; and that, as with the learning of foreign languages, conscious imitation is a stage of learning vital to the development of a voice which is not only competent, but individual.

Finally, a word about the key. When this book was piloted, students had to depend on their own observations from the very start: the way questions were framed against the primary material seemed to make this possible. Some students felt that my confidence undermined theirs. As a compromise, therefore, between encouraging the sort of independent learning which is necessary in today's academy and the need to give students support as they master the basic principles, I have included a key (suitably awkward to get at, human frailty being what it is) to the first two sections of the Core Element. Once those sections have been securely assimilated, the rest will be transparent.

Acknowledgements

This guide is rooted in my experience of teaching academic writing to non-native speakers of English, and (although they may be surprised to hear it) I owe a debt to staff of the Centre for English Language Studies, University of Birmingham, for opening my eyes to more systematic approaches to that task than I had imagined possible. A superb textbook for language teachers which I encountered at Birmingham, and which deserves to be better known among all those teaching writing, Michael McCarthy's *Discourse Analysis for Language Teachers* (CUP, 1991), pointed the way to useful sources of primary material. Colleagues at Worcester College of Higher Education have supplied interest and encouragement in ample measure. I am particularly grateful to those who have advised with the subject sections, and offer warm thanks to Debbie Sly (English), John Peters (History) and Erica Stratta (Sociology). A great deal of this book could not have been written but for the generosity of the students who offered work as the basis for samples. My only regret is that they all preferred the anonymity which I was obliged to offer. Behind everything, as always, have been Fiona, Joe and Madeleine, to whom this book is dedicated.

The author gratefully acknowledges the permission of the publishers Harper Collins to reprint an extract from Ninian Smart's *The Religious Experience of Mankind*, and that of Andre Deutsch Ltd to quote from *Social Sciences as Sorcery* by Stanislav Andreski.

PART I.
Core Elements

CORE ELEMENT 1:

Writing Paragraphs
About Problems and Solutions

Just to get you going, here are some samples of writing which aim to communicate the results of a new discovery in astronomy. Which do you think is the most effectively written, and why?

(a)   People used to have problems discovering all about other planets because they are so tiny compared to stars which are much bigger than the Earth, like the sun for example. Also, because planets don't give off light themselves they only only reflect it.

   Now though there's a way round this because Dr Campbell and his colleagues use high-resolution spectroscopy to show how the light from stars changes, this light changes because planets you can't see make them move.

(b)   An unseen planet can cause a star to be pushed or pulled out of its path, which causes the light emitted by the star to vary. It always used to be difficult to detect new planets partly because they are so much smaller than stars and partly because they don't, unlike stars, give off their own light. But if you can measure the variation in a star's light, as Dr Campbell and his team did with their high-resolution spectroscopy technique, you can get round the problem.

(c)   In the past, the search for other worlds has been hampered by two factors. First, planets are tiny objects compared with stars: for instance, the sun, a typical star, is 300,000 times more massive than the Earth. Second, planets do not shine but only reflect light dimly from stars.

   Dr Roger Campbell and his colleagues got round this problem by using high-resolution spectroscopy to measure accurately variation in a star's light. Slight differences in a star's light showed that many were being pushed and pulled out of their paths by unseen planets.

7

The passage you should have chosen was (c). In (a) there are badly constructed sentences, vague expressions, and a poor grasp of punctuation. Passage (b) uses more appropriate vocabulary but is not structured logically. Can you find some examples of such faults?

Now do the following exercises, based on passage (c), to explore what logical structure and appropriate language mean in practice. Here is passage (c) again:

In the past, the search for other worlds has been hampered by two factors. First, planets are tiny objects compared with stars: for instance, the sun, a typical star, is 300,000 times more massive than the Earth. Second, planets do not shine but only reflect light dimly from stars.

Dr Roger Campbell and his colleagues got round this problem by using high-resolution spectroscopy to measure accurately variations in a star's light. Slight differences in a star's light showed that many were being pushed and pulled out of their paths by unseen planets.

(The *Observer*, 5 July 1987, p.4)

Functions

1. You'll remember that we're dealing with a 'problem–solution' pattern, which is a common one in academic writing. Which paragraph of passage (c) deals with the problem, and which one with the solution?

2. The first paragraph of passage (c) contains three sentences, but two of them are doing the same job. What is that job?

3. What job is the remaining sentence of the first paragraph of passage (c) doing?

4. Now look at the second paragraph (of passage (c)). Which of the following describes the jobs performed by the two sentences in it?

   (i)   identify solution and give example of it
   (ii) identify solution and its application to the problem
   (iii) identify solution and re-state problem

Vocabulary and Grammar

5. Where in passage (c) could you insert the following, without changing the meaning?

    (i) which is
    (ii) themselves
    (iii) even

6. Which of the following could you use instead of 'hampered' (first sentence)?

    (i) made difficult
    (ii) interfered
    (iii) obstructed

7. Think of at least three words which you could use instead of 'got round', and at least another three which you could use instead of 'showed'.

8. What is the function of the colon (:) after 'compared with stars'?

    (i) it introduces specified additional information
    (ii) it ends the sentence
    (iii) it introduces a contrasting piece of information

9. Why is there an apostrophe in 'star's light'?

    (i) more than one star is being referred to
    (ii) it is an abbreviation for 'star is light'
    (iii) it indicates that the light belongs to the star

10. In passage (c), the construction 'do not... but only' ('planets do not shine but only reflect') is used to rule out an incorrect opinion. Using the same construction, rule out an incorrect opinion in your own field of study.

11. Re-write the sentence beginning 'Dr Roger Campbell' so that it begins with 'High-resolution spectroscopy'.

Writing to Format

12. We know that passage (c) is divided into paragraphs, and that each paragraph contains sentences doing different jobs. Look at the two sets of rough notes printed below, and write them up using the paragraph structure of passage (c).

(a) how to deal with hereditary diseases – agent carrying them unknown – technology not available to do anything even if known. Watson and Crick, 1953 – structure of DNA discovered – paved way for re-combinant technology – allows new genes to be inserted – replace defective ones.

(b) knowledge of social life in 17th century limited – only random records – letters, poems, government documents, etc. – much of this from aristocratic circles. Discovery of Pepys' diary – every day for ten years – ordinary things like eating, sleeping, work, sex, houses, servants.

Finished? From these brief examples you'll have learned that:

- paragraphs distinguish logically between aspects of a topic;
- paragraphs are structured, with each sentence doing a distinctive job.

Now for a slightly more substantial text.

All Western countries face a crisis in coping with the demands made on welfare provision by their growing elderly populations. The problem of resource scarcity is a real one. But perhaps not all countries have adopted so rigorously as Britain has the view that care should be based on the family model.

Scandinavia, for example, provides residential facilities for elderly people not wishing to remain at home or to live with their families, and those facilities are often available for use by local pensioners on a daily basis. Elderly people in the United States have developed communities of their own, supporting each other and running them by themselves, as their answer to increasing dependency. Some have argued against these 'age-dense' solutions, likening them to ghettos, but research suggests a high degree of consumer satisfaction.

Examples from other countries demonstrate that there are alternative ways of tackling the issues of caring and dependency. The family model of care with the high demands made on women and lack of choice and frequent loneliness for the dependents is not the only solution.

(New Society, 28 August 1987, p.12)

Functions

13. Overall, which is the 'problem' paragraph, and which the 'solution'?

14. How would you describe the job of the third paragraph? Does it:

    (i) summarise the content of the first two paragraphs?
    (ii) re-define some aspect of the problem?
    (iii) focus on the specific difficulties of one potential solution?

15. Look at the first paragraph. Like many orderly paragraphs in brief passages of this kind, it contains three sentences, each with a different function. How would you describe the functions of the first and third sentences?

16. What is sentence two doing there, sandwiched in the middle?

17. Now look at the second paragraph. The first two sentences share the same function. What is that?

18. How would you describe the function of the third sentence ('Some have argued...') in paragraph two?

    (i) illustrates an aspect of one solution
    (ii) raises an objection to a solution in order to dismiss it
    (iii) re-states the problem

Vocabulary and Grammar

19. Where in the passage could you insert the following without taking anything out? What difference would you make to the meaning if you did?

    (i) exclusively
    (ii) rapidly
    (iii) undoubtedly

20. Which of the following could you use instead of 'rigorously'?

    (i) mindlessly
    (ii) single-mindedly
    (iii) ruthlessly

21. 'Rigorously' is an adverb (a word that describes the way something is done), and 'rigorous' is an adjective (a word that describes an object or idea). There is also a noun, 'rigour'. What is the rule that tells you how to spell the adverb and adjective correctly? Think of some more examples like this.

22. In the second paragraph, the author places one phrase in inverted commas. Is this because:

    (i) it is a conventional or jargon phrase?
    (ii) it is being quoted from a book?
    (iii) it is not true?

23. What is the difference between 'adopting' a view and 'holding' a view?

24. Look at the sentence beginning 'Elderly people in the United States'. It falls into three parts:

    (i) Elderly people in the United States have developed communities of their own,
    (ii) supporting each other and running them by themselves,
    (iii) as their answer to increasing dependency.

    Can you describe the functions of the three parts?

25. Aspects of the solution are conveyed in the middle part of the sentence by two '-ing' forms: 'supporting each other and running them by themselves'. Now write a sentence based on the one above, using two or three '-ing' forms to illustrate aspects of a solution.

26. At the end of the first paragraph the author notes the special attention paid to a particular solution by Britain:

> not all countries have adopted so rigorously as Britain has the view that care should be based on the family model.

Using information from a field of study you're familiar with, write a sentence with the same structure.

27. Re-write the sentence beginning 'Elderly people in the United States' so that it begins 'Increasing dependency'.

Writing to Format

28. As you did with the spectroscopy passage, write up the following notes, basing your structure on the passage about welfare for the elderly. Try to write three sentences per paragraph.

> rising crime – every country – how to cope – British government building more prisons. Other options – Japan state subsides for jobs – people employed – France investment in community facilities – expensive but effective. Better long-term practice – ex-prisoners re-offend a lot

Core Element 2:
Sentences

In Core Element 1 you were asked to re-write some sentences, changing them round so that they began differently. This is an important exercise because:

- you often have to change the subject of a sentence to reflect the focus or emphasis of your argument;
- it gives you practice in using different constructions, so improving your understanding of the difference between good and bad grammar.

In this section you'll try some more exercises of this kind.

The rules of sentence construction in English would fill many books on their own. What we'll do here is focus on a fundamental distinction that causes students and (by extension) their tutors a lot of trouble: the difference between a *main clause* and a *subordinate clause*. Look at this sentence:

> In spite of the high price, George decided to buy the book because it would complete his collection, which was already the best in the country.

The principal action is 'George decided to buy the book'. Everything else depends on that action, and without it the sentence would have no meaning. By contrast, if you deleted either the first six words or the last eight there would still be a clear meaning. The principal action of the sentence, then, is the main clause, while everything is subordinate to it.

Main clauses can stand on their own as sentences: subordinate clauses cannot. It follows that the passages below all contain ungrammatical English:

(a) George decided to buy the book. In spite of the high price.
(b) George decided to buy the book, in spite of the high price. Because it would complete his collection.
(c) In spite of the high price, George decided to buy the book because it would complete his collection. Which was already the best in the country.

Often a main clause will be interrupted by other information:

George, in spite of the high price, decided to buy the book.

The principal action is still there, in spite of the distraction.

1. Now try underlining the main clause in each of the following sentences, bearing in mind that other clauses may be in the way:

(a)   Much as he liked hang-gliding, Malcolm hesitated to join his friends in their plan to glide off Ben Ormond at midnight, even though they urged him to come with them, because he considered it too dangerous.

(b)   Whenever Brian visited Bromyard he went straight to the old ironmonger's because he was sure he would find some bargains there, providing, of course, that the eccentric owner had remembered to open the shop.

(c)   In case the van broke down on the twisting mountain roads, which might mean that he would be attacked by the bandits who were known to live in the mountains and prey on travellers, especially those who were forced to spend the night there, Joe always carried a small motor bike in the back of his vehicle so that he could use it as a means of rapid escape if he had to.

(d)   Denise, whose elder brother, the European champion, had given her some coaching, hit the target again and again, whereas her fellow students, who hadn't any previous experience of the sport, usually missed, even after many hours' practice, much to the frustration of the instructor, who was doing his best to coach them.

(e) Fiona, who had never even been in a boat before coming on the course and, moreover, suffered from acute asthma, was, according to the instructors, one of the best divers they had ever had the pleasure of training.

2. Now try re-writing the sentences so that they begin like this (you must include all the information from the original sentence, and fit it all into a single sentence of your own; you may have to insert further phrases and punctuation):

   (a) Malcolm's friends...
   (b) The eccentric ironmonger...
   (c) Bandits living in the mountains...
   (d) The students in the class...
   (e) Fiona's instructors...

3. Now decide which of the following sentences are unacceptable, and write a correct version of each one you select:

(a)   In order to paint the wall, because it was extremely large, so the decorators used a special roller which enabled them to cover the most distant corners.

(b)   However hard he tried, James couldn't reach the standard necessary to pass his accountancy examination, so he decided to stop taking classes, even though he enjoyed them, and to devote much less time to study altogether.

(c)   When he first bought the house, because he didn't like the way it was decorated, although it took a long time and was expensive until it was re-decorated to his satisfaction.

(d)   They ran to a large tree, it was in the corner of the field, it sheltered them until the storm stopped.

(e)   In case you have a complaint, we want our customers to be satisfied so write to the address below, saying where you purchased the product and when.

(f)   The Duke accompanied the Queen to the aeroplane, wearing a cherry coat with matching hat and ear-rings.

CORE ELEMENT 3:
Writing Paragraphs
About Claims and Counter-claims

Like the problem–solution pattern, this is a common feature of academic writing. In every area of your work you will have to show that you understand the contrasting opinions of individuals or schools of thought. As before, there are two passages for you to work on. Here is the first:

> Local authorities believe strongly in the involvement of the public sector and the need for public planning. They think it is more important to protect jobs which are already in their area than to attract more from outside. In addition, since they hold that production is the key to economic revival, they think it is more important to sustain manufacturing industry than to switch to alternatives, such as the service industry.
>
> Central government, on the other hand, places more faith in the private sector for its schemes, and it considers that public planning hinders rather than helps redevelopment. It usually dismisses planning as 'red tape'. Government is also more interested in attracting new jobs than protecting old ones. Above all, it believes that the market decides what sort of jobs should and should not be done.
>
> (*New Society*, 28 August 1987, p.20)

Functions

1. Remember that we're dealing with the 'claim/counter-claim' pattern here. Each paragraph has an overall function. What is that function?

2. The first paragraph is, as in many short passages of this kind, a crisp three-sentence affair. Two of the sentences are doing a similar job. What is that job?

3. Can you divide up the second paragraph in the same way?

4. What sentence function is fulfilled by the last sentence of the passage?

Vocabulary and Grammar

5. Expressions such as 'believe', 'think', 'hold', 'places faith in' and 'interested in' signal a claim of one sort or another. Can you think of any other words that have the same function?

6. Look again at the following structures:

> (a) They think it is more important to... than to
> (b) considers that public planning hinders rather than helps
> (c) more interested in... than in

Using the terms 'claim' and 'counter-claim', define what function these structures have in the passage.

7. Now write down some sentences with similar structures, drawing on material from one of the subjects you're studying:

8. Now look again at the sentence beginning 'In addition...'. What function is being performed by the opening section of that sentence ('In addition... economic revival')?

   (i) expressing the consequences of the belief in manufacturing
   (ii) expressing the drawbacks of the belief in manufacturing
   (iii) expressing the reasons for the belief in manufacturing

9. Now write a similar sentence using material from a subject you're working on.

10. Which of the following could you use instead of 'on the other hand' (first sentence of paragraph two)?

    (i) notwithstanding
    (ii) by contrast
    (iii) nevertheless

11. In the phrase, 'for its schemes', the word 'its' has no apostrophe. Why?

    (i) because it means 'it is'
    (ii) because 'schemes' is in the plural
    (iii) because the schemes belong to the private sector

12. In the phrase, 'dismisses planning as "red tape"', what is the meaning of 'dismisses as'? Using material from one of your subjects, write a sentence using this expression.

13. In the first paragraph you find the expression, 'believe strongly in'. You will often find, instead, 'believe strongly that'. Re-write the first sentence so that it reads 'believe strongly that'.

14. Find the words or phrases in the passage that mean:

    (i) for example
    (ii) safeguard
    (iii) change
    (iv) dictates

15. Re-write the first sentence of the passage so that it begins 'Public planning...'.

Writing to Format

16. As you did with the problem–solution section, write your own passage using the rough notes provided below. Try to stay as close as possible to the pattern of the passage about local and central government. A crisp, two-paragraph account is what is needed. Change the phrasing as you think fit.

Bosnian conflict, 1994 – USA in favour of military action – air strikes, punishing perceived aggressors, shipping arms to Bosnian Muslims – belief that Serbs will withdraw if forced to – aid convoys to Bosnian citizens less important. EC countries value help to ordinary civilians – think military action provocative – air strikes don't help – arms to Muslims increase violence – diplomacy more likely to lead to a settlement.

Now for a slightly more extended passage. This one shows that the claim/counter-claim pattern is not confined to explicit disagreements:

Historians are generally agreed that British society is founded on a possessive individualism, but they have disputed the origins of that philosophy. Some trace it back to the Middle Ages, others link it to the rise of capitalism. But the consensus is that the cornerstone of this society has been the nuclear family – where man the breadwinner holds dominance over his dependent wife and chidren. The values of individual freedom, self-reliance, individual advancement and, crucially, the obligation of family duty to look after one's own in time of need, are central to its operation.

However, although most would accept that these values have been dominant, they would also acknowledge that the development of capitalist society saw the parallel growth of another ideology. Against individualism with its emphasis on individual freedom has been counterposed collectivism, with its egalitarian values and stress on the view that one individual's freedom cannot be paid for by the denial of freedom to others. The nineteenth-century growth of trade unions, the co-operative movement and organized socialist political movements are all evidence of this opposition to dominant ideology.

(*New Society*, 28 August 1987, p.10)

17. Describe the different functions of the two paragraphs.

18. Look at the first sentence of the passage, which introduces the topic. You will see that it is divided into two parts. Which of the following best describes the functions of the two parts of the sentence?

    (i) indicate field of consent; indicate field of disagreement
   (ii) indicate claim; indicate counter-claim
  (iii) indicate topic; indicate topics not dealt with

19. Now describe the function of the second sentence in relation to the first.

20. How about the third sentence?

21. And the fourth?

22. You have just worked out an outline of the first paragraph. Using the following rough notes, write a paragraph of your own which shares the structure of the 'Historians are generally agreed' paragraph.

> Ancient Greeks writers – study of language needed as part of study of philosophy. Controversy – What is a word? Just a social convention? Or part of the thing or person it describes? Agreed that it's hard to understand how we think without considering what words are. Ideas, concepts are based on words – different cultures have different words so different concepts.

23. Now look at the second paragraph of the 'Historians' passage. How would you describe the functions of its three sentences?

    (i) indicate counter-claim; specify counter-claim; re-define claim
   (ii) indicate counter-claim; give example of counter-claim; specify it
  (iii) indicate counter-claim; specify counter-claim; give example of it

Vocabulary and Grammar

24. Look at the first sentence of the second paragraph. It signals acceptance of two different claims, using the structure 'although

most would accept... they would also acknowledge'. Using material from a subject you're studying, write three sentences in the same format.

25. Look at the second sentence of paragraph two: 'Against individualism... has been counterposed collectivism...'. The subordinate clauses in the gaps (remember?), convey aspects of the claim and counter-claim: 'with its emphasis on individual freedom'; 'with its egalitarian values'. The overall structure of the sentence, then, is claim + aspect, counter-claim + aspect. Write a similar sentence using material you're familiar with.

26. Where in the passage could you insert the following without changing the meaning?

    (i) while
    (ii) often
    (iii) of them

27. List some other words you could use instead of:

    (i) crucially (first paragraph)
    (ii) founded on (first paragraph)
    (iii) advancement (first paragraph)
    (iv) parallel (second paragraph)
    (v) counterposed (second paragraph)
    (vi) dominant (second paragraph)

28. In the sentence beginning, 'However, although most would accept', the author twice uses the word 'would'. Why?

29. In the first paragraph there occurs the word 'dependent'. It is often hard to remember whether English words end with '-ant/ance' or '-ent/ence'. Which is the correct letter for the following? Have a go yourself first, and then use a dictionary.

resist-nt	independ-nt	flu-nt	appar-ntly
complim-nt	complem-nt	compli-nt	defend-nt
transcend-nt	curr-nt	pleas-nt	reli-nt
conting-nt	determin-nt	plang-nt	magnific-nt
domin-nt	segm-nt	expect-nt	pregn-nt
perman-nt	import-nt	evid-nt	rec-nt

Now look at the letter(s) preceding the a/e and see whether you can work out a rough rule for deciding cases like these.

30. Re-write the sentence beginning 'Historians are generally agreed', so that it begins 'The origins...'.

Writing to Format

31. Identify a controversy in one of your own subjects, where there are different explanations or views of something. Using the structures and functions of the 'Historians' passage as a model, write a two-paragraph account of the controversy.

Writing Brief Essays

So far we have dealt with relatively small segments of language: sentences and complementary paragraphs. That's because this is a step-by-step guide. Now it's time to think about managing larger structures. Again we will begin with some analysis. The mini-essay that follows concerns an entirely hypothetical (indeed, virtually nonsensical) topic; it's important at this stage for you to think about the process of writing rather than the content. There'll be plenty of time to think about the needs of your particular area of study when it comes to the subject-specific sections at the end of this book. The topic for this essay is:

Imagine that the government intends to bring in a law stating that everyone should live in apartments of exactly the same size. What would be the consequences, and would they be advantageous?

In most countries, people are used to seeing houses and apartments of many different shapes and sizes, made from a variety of materials, and reflecting the social and economic circumstances of the people who live in them. Such variety arguably makes life more interesting, as well as providing an index of people's control over their environment. But what if things were different? What if, as in some countries, everyone had to live in apartments of exactly the same size?

'Exactly the same *size*' – not necessarily apartments made of the same materials, furnished in the same way, or contained in identical buildings. The motive for such a law would be humane, not simply bureaucratic. There could be almost as much variety in the urban environment as there is now, but with a more even distribution of that scarce resource, space. Human beings are territorial creatures, so that an unfair distribution of space arouses envy and other undesirable, anti-social feelings. If living space were standardised, most people would feel happier with their lot, and be less inclined to worry about their status relative to others.

There would be a number of important practical consequences were a government bold enough to enact such a policy. People's social habits would change: fewer people would want to spend their leisure time at home, so bringing business to places of public entertainment, encouraging outdoor recreation, and fostering a greater sense of community, especially in larger towns. This, in turn, might bring about a general reduction in crime. There would be economic benefits, as well: greater efficiency in the use of domestic fuel (there could be definitive guidelines about how best to heat the home), growth in the construction industry, more work for people engaged in decorating and furnishing apartments, and so on. There would also be a greater concentration of living space, resulting in more land being available for recreation and agriculture. The advantages would be enormous.

Naturally, some unpleasant consequences would follow, but these would be outweighed by the benefits. People in larger houses would have to surrender some of their living space to accommodate other families, but they could be compensated for this by the government. Some historical buildings might have to be changed dramatically, but they could conceivably be retained as museums, with the people who lived in them being compelled by law to accept visitors. It is possible that there would be an overall decline in population, since people who wanted large families would be deterred by limitations on space, but this might be offset by the number of people given a permanent apartment for the first time who could then start families. All of these drawbacks would be negligible compared with the advantages.

Overall, if everyone lived in apartments of the same size there would certainly be greater social harmony and contentment. The example of countries such as Sweden and Japan, where inequalities of living space are much less evident, and where crime is much lower, underlines the benefits of standardisation. The losers from such a system would be those who could afford to lose, while society itself could only gain.

Functions

1. The structure of the essay depends on the principle that each paragraph has a function of its own. Identify the function of each paragraph.

2. You've probably described paragraph one as 'an introduction', or something of the sort. Let's think about what that word really

means. Which of the following best describes the function of the first paragraph?

(i) It states the author's opinion about the topic so that we know which point of view is going to be explored in the essay.
(ii) It shows how the question makes us look at things differently, sketching in a background to focus our attention.
(iii) It states a series of important facts about the topic to show that the author knows something about it.

3. Although the first paragraph is certainly 'introductory', so is the second. What function is being performed by the first sentence of the second paragraph?

(i) It picks up on the wording of the question in order to be precise about what is meant.
(ii) It explains how the author's opinion is relevant to an understanding of the question.
(iii) It demonstrates the author's opinions about alternative views of the topic.

4. Both the second and third paragraphs list the benefits of standardising living space, but there is a difference in the *kind* of benefits listed in each paragraph. What is that difference?

5. The fourth paragraph also uses the 'listing' mode, but this time in a different way. Look at the sentences beginning 'People in larger houses', 'Some historical buildings', and 'It is possible'. What function do they share?

6. Now write a similar sentence to the ones you've just looked at in question 5, using the rough notes below:

change appearance/character of old towns – more people live in centres – reduction in crime, vandalism etc

7. Below you will find the concluding paragraph of the sample essay re-printed, together with two alternative versions. Read each of them and compare what they set out to do:

(a)   Overall, if we all lived in apartments of the same size there would certainly be greater social harmony and contentment. The example of such countries as Sweden and Japan, where inequalities of living space are much less evident, and where crime is much lower, underlines the benefits of standardisation. The losers from such a system would be those who could afford to lose, while society itself could only gain.

(b)   In conclusion, there are a lot of arguments on either side of this question. It would be better for business, fuel efficiency, land use and the crime rate if everyone had to live in the same-sized apartments, but there would also be drawbacks: not as much variety, a decline in population, and so on on. Overall, it would be a good idea.

(c)   All in all, considerable benefits would accrue from such a policy. In addition to those mentioned above, there would be a stabilising of the property market, less money devoted to mortgages, and therefore more disposable income available for spending in the high street. This would lead to greater all-round prosperity.

Why did the author decide on version (a), do you think?

⚠️ *Remember to work through the Introductions and Conclusions sections of the subject-specific chapters of this book as well.*

Vocabulary and Grammar

8. You'll have noticed that the sample essay, because it deals with a hypothesis, uses a number of what are called *conditional* forms – could, would, etc. These are part of a larger class of expressions in English called *modals*, including will, shall, should, etc. The correct use of modals is essential if you are to signal accurately your commitment to a particular view or idea (we all know, after all, that 'I might come' means something very different from 'I will come'). Try re-writing the sentence you wrote in question 6 (page 26) a few times over, changing the modals in as many ways as you can so as to change the meaning.

9. Think of some other words or expressions that you could use instead of:

  (i) definitive (paragraph three)
  (ii) outweighed (paragraph four)
  (iii) negligible (paragraph four)
  (iv) inclined (paragraph two)
  (v) reflecting (paragraph one)

Writing to Format

10. Time for a very big breath, and an entire essay of your own. As before, make use of the structures and paragraph functions covered in this section (and previous ones). The question this time is even more daft than the last one, but it's the process that is important:

Imagine that the government brings in a law prohibiting the use of seats on buses. What would be the consequences, and would the move be beneficial?

The notes below will give you some help if you're completely bamboozled, but feel free to think up some ideas for yourself.

strange idea: purpose of transport is comfort – seatless trams and buses common in some countries. Old and disabled still taken care of.

good things: more people in one bus – cheaper to run buses – lower ticket prices – more people leave cars at home – easier and cheaper to clean buses – more pleasant to use – no seats to vandalise & therefore repair – no conflict over who should have the one seat left.

bad things: difficult for old/disabled people – inconvenient for shoppers – potentially dangerous in sudden stops/sharp corners – overcrowding more likely – some people put off by discomfort – more people on a bus might mean fewer buses in a day – most people would prefer comfort – force old and disabled people out of their seats.

Writing Summaries

An essential skill which you will have to master is that of summary. One of your tutors may ask you to summarise an article for oral or written presentation, and whenever you write an essay you will certainly need a clear sense of other people's approaches to your topic. Acquiring skills in summary will also help you to cope with the volume of reading in your chosen course since, if you know how to look for crucial information, you will be able to find it more quickly.

As before, we'll begin with some reading. The piece below is about the introduction of Buddhism to China. It is then summarised in three different ways. Think about which summary is the most successful, and why.

The introduction of Buddhism into China probably dates from the first century AD. The Han emperor Ming is said to have had a dream in which there appeared a golden man, which was interpreted as a reference to the Buddha. Ming is supposed to have despatched envoys to northwest India to bring back information and scriptures. There are reasons to think that this story is merely a myth, but there is evidence of the existence of Buddhist monks and laymen in China in AD 65. The route by which these people and ideas reached China was that of the Central Asian silk roads. During the period in question a great slice of northern India, including much of modern Pakistan, together with modern Afghanistan and a large section of what are now the Central Asian republics of the U.S.S.R., was controlled by the Kushan empire.

Because of imperial patronage, Buddhism was enabled to spread easily throughout this area, and this brought it into contact with peoples and cultures of the places along the silk route. In this way it was possible for it to penetrate eastwards into northwestern China. Probably in the early days of this peaceful invasion of China, Buddhism became the faith of traders, merchants and shopkeepers, and did not spread much to the native Chinese population. Nevertheless, it

---

established itself in the imperial capital of Loyang, and missionary monks came there to recommend the religion. The work of translating Indian texts into Chinese was commenced – an immense undertaking – so that by the second century AD Buddhism was definitely beginning to make its contribution to Chinese culture. The spread of Buddhism was assisted by the disintegration of the Han empire toward the latter part of that century. In a time of turbulence, civil war, and unrest, the official Confucian doctrines were bound to seem ineffective and inadequate, and the way was open for a faith which had more personal and individual concerns.

Early in the process of introducing Buddhism to China, the texts translated were Lesser Vehicle ones, but the bulk of the texts translated later were Mahayana. It was this form of Buddhism which was to dominate in China, though it in turn was influenced by native elements in the culture which it permeated.

The appeal of the new faith was various. First, the monastic order – the Sangha – presented an ideal of the contemplative and religious life which could command respect. Moreover, the order was open to all, and thus provided a peaceful haven for many for whom the bloodshed and distresses of the period had become intolerable. The notion that a person should forsake his kith and kin to lead a religious life undoubtedly encountered considerable resistance in a culture where family ties, reinforced by the cult of ancestors, were so strong. Nonetheless, the Sangha gradually made headway.

Second, and equally important, one could be a good Buddhist without actually entering the order. The layman, as we saw in an earlier chapter, was given hope and comfort in the Mahayana to a degree that was impossible according to the Lesser Vehicle doctrines. The idea that the layman, by calling on the name of the Buddha, could have assurance that his next re-birth would be in paradise (the Pure Land of the West) and thereby a fine chance in the next world of attaining Nirvana, gave Buddhism a strong appeal among those who felt the call of popular devotion but not that of the strictly monastic life. Moreover, this notion of re-birth in paradise effectively short-circuited the doctrine of reincarnation. The thinking of Mahayana Buddhism did not so strongly depict an individual existence as stretching endlessly forward in a series of human and animal lives. This was important to the success of Mahayana piety in a culture that did not have belief in re-birth.

Another factor in the spread of Buddhism in China is a general one which helps to account for its spread elsewhere. Buddhism may be agnostic about the existence of a supreme Creator, and its doctrines may centre on the quest for release – the peace and serenity attainable in Nirvana – but it has never felt it necessary to deny popular religion. The gods, spirits, and demons that people the world of the ordinary folk in the lands to which Buddhism has come, including India, are not rejected. They are part of the furniture of the cosmos in which we live. There is no great harm in worshipping such spirits, so long as it is recognized that the highest salvation comes through following the way of the Buddha. Buddhism has tamed, rather than eradicated, such popular religion. Thus, in China, Buddhism felt no motive to protest against the cult of ancestors or to wipe out the cults of popular deities.

Buddhist ritual provided a powerful rival to that of the Confucianists and Taoists. By the time Buddhism penetrated into China, the cult of images of the Buddha was already well established. The magnificent sculpture of northwest India was imported too along the silk routes. The serene figures of Gautama and the graphic paintings of Bodhisattvas and celestial Buddhas combined to convey in impressive form the two dimensions of the new faith – the abstraction and serenity of one who has won his way to nirvana and the beneficent power of celestial forces to give salvation to the worshipper.

It should be recognized that Buddhism had its darker message. The Pure Land to which the faithful might be translated and the other paradises of popular teaching were complemented by the purgatories, often depicted in the most grisly and terrifying ways, in which evil men would have to work off their sins. Thus Buddhism provided vivid supernatural sanctions for good conduct in a way that was largely absent in earlier Chinese beliefs.

(*The Religious Experience of Mankind*, Ninian Smart,
New York, 1969, pp.220–22)

Sample Summaries

Try to decide which of these is the most successful, and why. (Each one occupies the same number of lines.)

(a)   China was introduced to Buddhism in about the first century AD, after the Han emperor Ming, having had a dream in which he saw a golden man, sent envoys to India to bring back information about the Buddha. Buddhist monks and believers appeared in China in AD 65, having travelled along the silk road, which was opened up to them because large parts of India, Pakistan, Afghanistan and the Soviet

Union were under the same empire at that time. The first Chinese Buddhists were mostly businessmen or traders, apart from in the capital, and monks started to translate Buddhist scriptures into Chinese, so that by the second century AD, a time of great disturbance because of the collapse of the Han empire and all the unrest which followed, the new religion had quite a strong hold and contributed a great deal to native Chinese culture through emphasising the personal and individual aspects of human life. Some of the other reasons why the new religion succeeded were: being a Buddhist monk was attractive; it appealed to ordinary people; Buddhism was not monotheistic, and boasted impressive statues; and it did threaten punishment to sinners, unlike other established religions.

(b)   Buddhism became popular in China for a number of reasons. First, its emphasis on the personal and individual aspects of life contrasted appealingly with the more social orientation of Confucianism at a time of social unrest deriving from the decline of the Han empire. Second, it presented a positive image of life in a monastery, offering the opportunity for calm and meditation away from the violence of contemporary life. Third, Buddhism embraced ordinary people as well as those who wanted to become monks, because individual believers were given the prospect of salvation in the next world, not simply reincarnation, in which the Chinese did not believe in any case. Fourth, because Buddhists do not assert that the world was made by one God, emphasising instead the release from suffering in this world, they do not attempt to challenge native religious traditions: long-standing local and national cults were allowed to sit alongside Buddhism without threat. Fifth, Buddhist sculptures conveyed an attractive message of both salvation and kindness, which contrasted with Taoist and Confucian images. Finally, Buddhism's threats of punishment for sinners gave an extra incentive for behaving well.

(c)   Buddhism probably reached China in the first century AD. The story goes that the emperor Ming dreamed of a golden man (the Buddha) and sent envoys to India to collect information and scriptures, but Buddhists were definitely in China by AD 65, most of them traders along the silk road. Monks came to the capital, Loyang, translated scripture (mostly of the Mahayana form of Buddhism) into Chinese, and so began to make available to native people harried by unrest a religion that reassuringly emphasized personal concerns over social ones. Buddhism appealed to the Chinese because its monastic element was an attractive alternative to the bloodshed of recent years, progressing even in a country which traditionally frowned on the

renunciation of family ties. Moreover, salvation was possible in
Mahayana Buddhism even for lay believers, since re-birth into Nirvana
was favoured over the chain of reincarnation, in which the Chinese had
never believed. Buddhist tolerance of popular forms of worship has
always helped its cause, while the serenity and beneficence of its icons
heightened its appeal over Confucian and Taoist ritual. Its threats of
punishment in the afterlife enhanced its moral claims.

Have you any views about how the three authors went about their
task?

The summary you should have preferred was (c). Summary (a) is
very unbalanced: it says far more about the beginning of the passage,
misses out some of the attractions of Buddhism to first century
Chinese people, and is stylistically deficient (one crucial error is that
it fails to reflect the sceptical mode of the first paragraph, treating
as facts what the author of the passage records as legends). Summary
(b) goes straight for the attractions of Buddhism without mentioning
the circumstances of its introduction to China, and plods through
them in a mechanical way with no regard for their relationship or
scale of importance as envisaged by the original author. Summary
(c) spends more time on the reasons for the appeal of Buddhism to
which the original author gave priority. More on these drawbacks
below. Summary (c) is not perfect: there are arguably some pertinent
facts missing, but then a summary has to exclude something in order
to be a summary!

Gathering Information

You'll know by now that the purpose of a paragraph is to contain a
particular aspect of the overall topic. It follows that if you want to
summarise what someone else has written, you should think first of
all about the way the paragraphs are arranged.

1. What aspect of the subject of Buddhism in China is dealt with
   in each of the paragraphs of the original passage?

2. Very often the aspect of the subject with which an individual
   paragraph is concerned will be signalled by what is called a

'topic sentence'. A topic sentence announces or sums up the main purpose of the paragraph. It won't always come at the beginning, or at the end; sometimes a topic-signalling function will be divided between two sentences. You can help yourself to read in a more alert and accurate manner by getting some practice in spotting topic sentences. Identify what you take to be the topic sentences in each of the paragraphs in the original passage.

3. Did you find some paragraphs where there was a problem finding the topic sentence? Bear in mind that topic sentences are a useful but not infallible guide to the content of a paragraph.

Translating Information

4. Sumarising doesn't just mean, for example, writing down all the topic sentences in their original order. As with essays, you need to consider questions of relationship and priority. Try mapping your answers from question 1 (above) on to summary (c). Write the numbers i–vii next to the relevant parts of the summary, as you think fit.

5. Were there any problems? You should have found that the order has changed. The author of summary (c) has shifted material around in order to make sense of the original in a different format. Find some examples of where this has happened.

6. Remember that a good summary, like a good essay, will always try to bring out the relationship between one paragraph and another.

Getting the Author's Attitude Right

7. When you are asked to summarise a piece of writing, you have to capture not only facts and their explanations, but opinions and arguments. You've just encountered one example of the problems involved here. Summary (a) suggests that the original author is less sceptical than he really is about key features of

his account. Identify the words or phrases in the first paragraph of the passage which distinguish between known fact and conjecture or legend, and then identify the words or phrases in summary (c) which do the same.

8. Very often an author will reveal an attitude by discounting an alternative explanation or opinion. It follows that if you are to get the author's attitude right, it is very important to distinguish between an opinion quoted in order to be rejected and one that is quoted for approval. Read the following passages carefully.

(a) Following the Second World War in the United States, there was something that could be called the free enterprise or market revival. It deeply engaged the conservative mind. Our conservatism is normally thought to depend on self-interest, moral indignation, vehement expression, and something approximating to religious revelation. This is unjust. The influence of ideas cannot be excluded anywhere.
(*The Affluent Society*, JK Galbraith, London, 1969, p.9)

(b) Chomsky contended that the child is born with an innate predisposition towards language, and that this innate property is universal in all human beings. This 'innateness hypothesis' was a possible resolution between behaviourism, which asserts that language is a set of habits acquired by conditioning, and the obvious fact that such conditioning is much too slow and inefficient a process to account for the acquisition of a phenomenon as complex as language. But the innateness hypothesis presented a number of problems itself.
(*Principles of Language Learning and Teaching*, H Douglas Brown, Englewood Cliffs NJ, 1987, p.27)

(c) Many psychologists criticize the administration of justice based on the idea of free will and responsibility without realizing that, if valid, determinism applies to everybody: if a criminal cannot avoid committing a crime, then neither can the judge avoid sentencing him, nor can the executioner avoid quartering him. Unless we assume that individuals can make decisions, and are responsible for at least some of their deeds, there is no reason why we should regard any action as good or bad, or try to refrain from doing harm.
(*Social Sciences as Sorcery*, Stanislav Andreski, Harmondsworth, 1974, p.23)

Now write down the words and phrases that convey the authors' disagreement with the opinions being quoted.

9. For each passage, summarise briefly the view that is being challenged, and (where possible) the author's own position.

Writing to Format

10. Now for another deep breath (you're close to the end of the core element now!), and some work on your own, full-length summary. Read the following passage carefully and, making use of the skills you have encountered in this section, write a summary of it in no more than 150 words.

All institutions devoted to the pursuit of knowledge face an inescapable dilemma: if authority is vested in professional administrators we get a situation in which the blind are telling the seers where to go, whereas if scientists and scholars have to undertake the task of management, they often turn into sterile neuters who can neither administer efficiently nor discover anything worthwhile. The universities which have the best record as centres of creativity have during that time succeeded in maintaining a delicate balance between the respective burdens and powers of the two breeds of men, with the aid of such devices as rotation in office, or the employment in supreme administrative posts of people well past the peak of creativity but whose record shows that they know from personal experience what intellectual creation involves and demands. Such compromises between very different types of ability and mentality, however, remain feasible only in fairly small institutions; and growth to a mammoth size inevitably entails a thorough bureaucratization.

On the Continent, control over the universities is vested not even in the internal administration but in the ministry of education, which vets examinations and textbooks – which is, I think, one of the main reasons why these countries have fallen behind Britain and the United States, where universities are much freer, in scientific and scholarly production. The disadvantage of the British way of running a university is that it tends to turn scientists and scholars into full-time administrators as soon as they reach a professorship, whereas the common American solution has been to give power to professional managers often drawn from business. This largely accounts for the alienation of the teachers, which aggravates the students.

I would venture a hypothesis that there is a significant negative correlation between the quality of a university (as measured by the contributions to knowledge by its staff and former students in proportion to their numbers) and the extent of the power wielded by professional managers. This relationship is obscured by the differences in size, which give people an illusion that the big centres are better because they contain a larger number of eminent scientists and scholars, although in relation to the total membership they may compare unfavourably with much smaller institutions. It does not follow, for example, that either Russia or the United States is better than Finland in sport by virtue of having more Olympic champions, because to get a true picture we would have to take the size of the populations into account. Similarly, people get exaggerated ideas about the excellence of the United States in science, which can be corrected by the following rough calculations. Among Nobel Prize winners, 79 were American and 46 British, which gives a net superiority to Britain if calculated in relation to the population, even apart from the fact that a much larger part of the American winners were born and educated abroad. In relation to the money spent on higher education the British production of Nobel Prize winners is about 12 times greater.

Serious as it is, owing to its tendency to favour staleness and mediocrity, the internal bureaucratization of the universities pales into insignificance as an obstacle to the progress of scholarship and science in comparison with the paramount importance of censorship. In an earlier chapter I have dealt with the more devious methods of restricting freedom of thought; and I do not need to go to great lengths to adduce evidence for the obvious truth that even without other forms of pressure, official pressure alone can suffocate science. What does call for some comment, however, is the seldom mentioned fact that intellectual freedom flourishes over a much smaller part of the globe today than in 1900, despite the vast increase in the numbers of universities, learned associations and libraries.

(*Social Sciences as Sorcery*, Stanislav Andreski, Harmondsworth, 1974, p.23)

CORE ELEMENT 6:
References and Bibliographies

All academic writers have to learn to compile accurate bibliographies and give proper references for information they use from books, articles and other sources. If you don't, the person marking your essay may conclude either that you haven't bothered to find out about the topic, or that you have filched everything you've written without declaring it.

Unfortunately, there are different conventions for recording this kind of information. Your best bet is stick consistently to one which you know is approved. The exercises below deal with two common ways of recording sources. As before, the principle is that you're more likely to learn rules by observation, deduction and imitation than by being told.

Bibliographies

1. A bibliography is a list of all the books you have consulted for a particular piece of work. You write it at the end of the essay. Here are two common ways of making such a list:

(a) Bowers, T.K.	*Investigations into Metaphysics*	(Oxford, 1990)
Carruthers, F.	*The Problem of Meaning*	(London, 1988)
——	*Weber in Context*	(Cambridge, 1986)
Prorty, G.M.	*The Social and Society*	(Sydney, 1987)
Richardson, B., & Ryan, A.	*Readings in Ethnology*	(London, 1971)

(b) Bowers, T.K. (1990)	*Investigations into Metaphysics*	(Oxford)
Carruthers, F. (1988)	*The Problem of Meaning*	(London)
—— (1986)	*Weber in Context*	(Cambridge)
Prorty, G.M. (1987)	*The Social and Society*	(Sydney)
Richardson, B., & Ryan, A. (1971)	*Readings in Ethnology*	(London)

Format (b), confusingly enough, is often referred to not as a bibliography, but as a list of references. Social scientists in particular prefer this mode of presentation. We'll clear that one up in a minute. Each example contains the *minimum* information you should give in a bibliography: you can include the author's given name and the publisher if you wish. What are the rules for recording the authors' names in these minimum lists?

2. What are the rules for recording the title of a book?

Now look at these bibliography entries, consisting of articles from learned journals:

(a) Boffer, D. 'A New Approach to the Phatic', *Communication Studies* 56 (1988), pp.67–98

Christopher, G. 'Reduced Vowel Variation in the North of England', *Language and Society* 44 (1990), pp.101–21

Grindling, K.R. 'Towards a Poetics of Rap', *South Carolina Studies in Popular Literature* 4 (1991), pp.34–45

—— 'Kitteredge's Dilemma and the Poetics of Rap', *South Carolina Studies in Popular Literature* 6 (1993), pp.1–35

Johnson, M. 'Notes on British Rap', *Popular Culture* 18, vol 3 (Autumn 1994), pp.16–30

Kitteredge, B. 'Grindling, Rap, and Post-Modernism', *South Carolina Studies in Popular Literature* 5 (1992), pp.56–89

(b) Boffer, D. (1988) 'A New Approach to the Phatic', *Communication Studies* 56, pp.67–98

Christopher, G. (1988) 'Reduced Vowel Variation in the North of England', *Language and Society* 44, pp.101–21

> Grindling, K.R. (1991) 'Towards a Poetics of Rap', *South
>   Carolina Studies in Popular Literature* 4, pp.34–45
> —— (1993) 'Kitteredge's Dilemma and the Poetics of Rap', *South
>   Carolina Studies in Popular Literature* 6, pp.1–35
> Johnson, M. (1994) 'Notes on British Rap', *Popular Culture* 18,
>   vol 3 (Autumn issue), pp.16–30
> Kitteredge, B. (1992) 'Grindling, Rap, and Post-Modernism',
>   *South Carolina Studies in Popular Literature* 5, pp.56–89

3. What are the rules for recording the title of an article?

4. What are the rules for recording the title of the journal containing the article?

5. What are the rules about recording volume and page numbers?

6. Now look at the following bibliography, which has been compiled by an exceptionally careless student. There are more than twelve mistakes – see if you can spot them.

Gordon O'Reilly	The Last of the Cherokees	(Indiana, 1990)
Pierce, R A	*Nine journeys round Africa*	London 1900
Quigley, D.	*The Struggle for Okinawa*	(Tokyo, 1987)
Rees, P.	*The Piper Alpha Disaster*, 'Modern Ecology' 22, 1993	
Aldine, A.	'Science Fiction and Ecology', *Studies in the Ecology of the Eighteenth Century* 34 (1983), p.12–27	
Walters, I., (and Smith)	*Studies in the Nucler Family* (London, 1980)	

7. By now you should be in command of the basics. There are, however, many categories of bibliographical item that have rules of their own. Look at the following entries, and work out how they are different from what you've covered so far. Make a note of any new rules as you go along.

Hughes, F. 'Theme and Structure in *Romeo and Juliet*', *Studies in Shakespeare* 45 (1976), pp.67–78

McManaway, H. 'Bush and the Abortion Question', in Millard, R., ed., *American Politics in the 1990s* (Columbia, 1994), pp.167–201

Stevens, W. '"I have a dream": King and Civil Rights', *Texas Studies in History* 21 (1981), pp.12–17

Pilkington, V. *The Natural History of the Giraffe* ed. M. Day (London, 1977)

Pilkington, V. *The Natural History of the Giraffe* (Cambridge, 1900)

Day, M. Introduction to Pilkington, V., *The Natural History of the Giraffe* (London, 1977)

Shakespeare, W. *Romeo and Juliet*, directed by Cedric Messina (BBC Videos, 1978)

Jay, P. 'Five Justifications for the ERM', *The Independent* 24th January 1988, p.12

Anderson, P. 'Greek Architecture', *Encyclopaedia Britannica* 24 vols (London, 1969), vol 7. pp.207–14

One last thing to bear in mind. Some subject disciplines, such as English and History, often divide a bibliography into two halves: one for **primary texts** (the literary or documentary material which forms the focus of discussion); the other for **secondary texts** (critical discussions of those texts).

Referencing

8. Proper referencing shows that you have acknowledged the contribution of other minds to your work. Look at some of the different ways of doing that:

(a)   In Dickinson's view, 'Purcell's contribution to the development of opera was seminal', prompting a more imaginative use of recitative and chorus among dozens of rivals and imitators (3).

(b)   Thomas Dickinson argued that Purcell was a crucial figure in the development of opera, leading other composers to treat recitative and choral sections with considerably greater freedom and dramatic effectiveness (7).

(c) In Thomas Dickinson's view,
> Purcell's contribution to the development of opera was seminal, an inspiration to subsequent generations of composers suddenly able to treat recitative and choral work with a sense of drama unthought of in the previous history of the genre (35).

(d) After all, as Dickinson (1983) observed, 'Purcell's contribution to the development of opera was seminal, an inspiration to subsequent generations of composers suddenly able to treat recitative and choral work with a sense of drama unthought of in the previous history of the genre' (p.16).

The last example normally goes with the author (date) style of bibliography you encountered a couple of pages back as format (b), which you'll recall is the sort of bibliography usually termed 'References'. Leaving that aside, note down some rules for acknowledging the wisdom of Professor Dickinson and any other sources you might use (you'll have noticed that Dickinson's words are found on page 16 of his book, and not pages 3, 7 or 35, which belong to the essay-writers' different number sequences).

9. Examples (a), (b) and (c) presuppose a list of references either at the end of the essay, before the bibliography, or at the bottom of the page where they occur. At the bottom of the Dickinson-on-opera page, for example, you might find the following:

35. F. Dickinson, *The Development of English Opera* (London, 1983), p.16.

How is this different from a bibliography entry?

10. A list of references of the sort that comes before a bibliography might look like this:

---

1. M.C. Margeson, *Life in Rural Japan* (New York, 1954), p.56
2. R. Ripley, *Economic Planning in East Asia*, 1960–80 (London, 1985), p.67
3. Margeson, op.cit., p.45
4. Ibid., p.206
5. Ibid., p.200
6. J. Davidson, *Poverty and the Burakumin in Modern Japan* (Oxford, 1987), p.203
7. Ibid., p.176
8. Margeson, op.cit., p.155
9. Ripley, *The Tiger Economies* (London, 1990), pp.45–6

What are the rules for recording authors' names?

11. When should you use 'op.cit.' and 'ibid.'?

12. Remember that none of this is necessary when you use the author (date) style of format (b). Just give the page reference after each quotation. But what has happened to the date here?

As Johnstone (1987ii) observes, this must be 'the more persuasive view' (p.66).

The answer, of course, is that Johnstone is a very productive author. With this system, the same notation should be used in the complete list of references at the end (ie in what is otherwise known as a bibliography), so that the reader knows which of the fecund Johnstone's many 1987 publications is meant: 1987i, 1987ii, or 1987iii, and so on.

13. Test your findings against a variety of academic books.

Using references: a warning

Acknowledging other people's contributions to your work is not all you do when you write. You must also think about the validity of their evidence and reasoning. Look for controversy, not just support:

quote authors who disagree with each other, and with whom you disagree. Don't just report – argue. There's more about this in the subject sections (p.90).

Abusing references: a warning

Reproducing material without acknowledgement is often called plagiarism, and plagiarism, when detected, will land you in trouble. You will recall the Dickinson passage on Purcell a couple of pages back:

> Purcell's contribution to the development of opera was seminal, an inspiration to subsequent generations of composers suddenly able to treat recitative and choral work with a sense of drama unthought of in the previous history of the genre.

Here are four *unacceptable* ways of transmitting Professor Dickinson's wisdom. Read them carefully and compile a list of things you should avoid.

> (a)   Dickinson claims that 'Purcell's contribution to the development of opera was seminal' (1). It was an inspiration to subsequent generations of composers suddenly able to treat recitative and choral work with a sense of drama unthought of in the previous history of the genre.
>
> (b)   Purcell's contribution to opera inspired subsequent generations of composers who could suddenly treat recitative and choral work with a sense of drama unthought of in the previous history of the genre. The contribution he made was seminal.
>
> (c)   Purcell made a major contribution to opera, according to Dickinson. He inspired subsequent generations of composers who were suddenly able to treat recitative and choral work with a sense of drama unthought of in the previous history of the genre.
>
> (d)   Purcell's contribution to the development of opera was seminal, an inspiration to subsequent generations of composers suddenly able to treat recitative and choral work with a sense of drama unthought of in the previous history of the genre (3).

You will probably have realised that it could be quite easy to steal material without exactly meaning to: you're making notes from a book, don't record the references, and then, when you come to write up the notes, you come to an attractive sentence or paragraph which you decide to use. It goes straight into your essay as you found it. This too is a kind of plagiarism. Remember to write down all references as you take notes and you won't be caught unawares.

Core Element 7:
Proofreading

Appropriately enough, this is the last section of the Core Element. Nothing annoys a marker more than an essay full of careless errors. It is your responsibility to check for presentational mistakes before you hand your work in. Check everything: spelling, punctuation, referencing, the lot. What follows is a passage from a carelessly prepared essay. Find and mark as many errors as you can, and then see where you stand as a proofreader on the scale given below.

Our attitudes to animals begin to form when we are very young, and they dominated by the fact that we begin to eat meat at a very early age (1). Interestingly enough, many children at first refuse to eat animal flesh, and only became accustomed to it after strenuos efforts by there parents, who mistakenly believe it is neccesary for good health. What ever the childs initial reaction, however, the point to notice that we eat animal flesh long before we are capable of understanding that what we eat is the body of a dead amimal (2). Thus we never make a consciuos, enformed decision, free from bias that enforms any long-established habit, re-inforced by all the pressures of social conformity, not to animal flesh. At the same time, children have a natural love of animals, and our society encourages them to affectionate towards pets and cuddly stuffed toy animals. From these facts stem the most distictive characteristic of the attitude of children in our society to animals – namely, that there is not infact one unified attitude to animals, but two conflicting attitudes which co-exist in one individual, carefully segregated so that the inherant contravention between them rarely causes trouble (4).

SCALE
20: Keep it up!
17–19: Some improvement desirable.
0–16: Pretty rusty. Be more vigilant!

46

PART II.
Marking and Essays

Marking Criteria
For Degree-level Work

This is essential reading if you are to understand the principles on which your work is marked. Read the marking criteria carefully and think particularly about the phrases in italics. You will need to bear these in mind when you work through the sample essays in each subject section. It will be useful to think about which of the criteria reflect comments that have been made about your written work in the past, or that correspond to your own sense of your strengths and weaknesses as a writer.

Grade A

The work will be outstanding, showing clear evidence of *originality, liveliness* and *enthusiasm*. It will reveal clear and comprehensive *knowledge* and *understanding* of the topic of study and appropriate technical expertise together with the ability to bring *fresh perspectives* to the module objectives. Initiative in study will be evident from the use of primary and secondary sources, and from the *collection, selection, presentation* and *analysis* of appropriate data. Depth of study will be matched by the ability to incorporate imaginative references that *set the work in a broader context*.

The response will be *directly relevant to the given topic*, organised systematically around a *central argument* or *theme* and confidently located within an *appropriate conceptual framework*. It will offer an effective synthesis of all the ideas and materials presented, including *personal departures from existing scholarly theory*. It will be sensitive to the *claims of various theoretical positions* while making *firm and independent judgments* in its conclusions. The ideas will be *communicated effectively, with economy and precision*, using *language appropriate to the academic discipline or disciplines*. The work will conform to the highest standards of scholarship in its presentation, including impeccable referencing and a comprehensive bibliography.

Grade B

Work at this level will be distinguished by *some independence of thought*. It will show a good knowledge and understanding of the relevant material, both primary and secondary, and a high level of competence in handling data and in practical skills. Some ability to set the work *in a broad framework of reference* will be evident, though *without the confident grasp of wider issues characteristic of Grade A answers*. The typical response will be *fully elaborated and coherent* with a *well-constructed and clear central argument* and evidence of *wide and intelligent reading*, while not being as perceptive as Grade A work. *Some original critical insight* may be developed but, on the whole, while making a *sound synthesis of varying interpretations*, the work will show *less independent judgment* and insight and have a tendency to be *comprehensive rather than penetrating*. Written work will *use appropriate language correctly* and will be *well presented* in terms of scholarship.

Grade C

Work in this category will show a *straightforward conceptualisation of the topic* rather than a critical or sophisticated one. There will be evidence of a *competent grasp* of module objectives and of an ability to *locate the central issues* and understand their importance. *Sufficient reading* and other preparation will have been undertaken to handle the topic with reasonable confidence though there will be a tendency towards *the uncritical assimilation of ideas*. Background knowledge and understanding will be generally satisfactory. The typical answer will be *an adequate, though restricted response*, based upon *sound, careful and competent work*. It is likely to be *descriptive rather than analytical*, not using evidence to its best effect and *lacking critical perception*. It will be competently written, although with *quotations used as a substitute for original thought*.

Grade D

The work will be of an adequate standard showing *basic knowledge, skill and understanding*. Most of the main points will be covered, but the response will be heavily dependent on received opinion and a very limited range of resources. There will be *little or no evidence of initiative in reading and collection of appropriate data.* The work will, for the most part, show acceptable organisation and sense of purpose, though *the control of argument may be lost at certain points.* Language use will be at the minimum acceptable level, showing *imprecision, some carelessness,* and *little command of technical language.* The apparatus of scholarship may be misused or neglected.

Fail Grades E & F

Work of this standard will show *some knowledge of the topic* and field of study. *Understanding of major issues will be incomplete,* however, and there will be *little evidence of relevant reading and study.* The answer will be based on *inadequate data, lacking a coherent structure of argument* and failing to address itself directly to the question. Written work is likely to make *sweeping, sometimes erroneous generalisations,* and to show an *unacceptable level of literacy,* with naive or *ungrammatical sentence structure, mishandling of data* and *spelling mistakes.* It is likely to be *careless* and *indifferent to matters of presentation.* Grades E or F will be awarded according to the extent of the drawbacks identified here, and the scope of the knowledge displayed.

Essays in English and Literary Studies

Sample Essays

What follows is a sample of essays submitted by first-year students of English over the past few years. There are four essays, on different subjects, and each one gained a different pass mark, from A to D. Satisfy yourself that you're familiar with the marking criteria given in the previous section and then read through all the essays, trying to decide which essay gained which mark. You might like to make a note of any sections or passages that fulfil particular aspects of the criteria, or which seem to you especially successful or unsuccessful for any other reasons. Think, for example, about how well the essay answers the question set. After the essays, there are some exercises for you to look at.

> ⚠ *No end-notes are included in these samples, although the numbers are given in the body of each piece. You should never neglect referencing in your own work!*

—1—

QUESTION: It has been suggested that in *Jane Eyre* Charlotte Brontë aims at a 'union of realism and romance' (King). Examine the structure and meaning of the novel in the light of this claim.

The structure of the novel *Jane Eyre* may be divided into several parts, each one conducive to the growth, both morally and emotionally, of the main character. Jane's progress has been suggested as parallel to Bunyan's *Pilgrim's Progress*. (1) However, Jane's progress is not for the heavenly hereafter so much as finding heaven here on earth. Jane seeks her true identity and learns that the passion within her is equal to any man's. Charlotte Brontë wrote, 'Women are supposed to be very calm generally; but women feel just as men feel; they need exercise for their faculties and a field for their efforts as much as their brothers do.' (2)

The tension between realism and romance in the novel has been suggested as a metaphor for the workings of the novel's structure. (3) This tension is seen in the opening of the first chapter. Orphaned and moneyless, Jane survives life with the bullying Reed family; by hiding behind closed curtains, immersed in fairy tales and travel books, she loses herself in her vivid imagination. John Reed is a powerful and realistic portrayal of snobbery and self-centredness. The social gap that is shown towards Jane by the Reed family is the setting for Jane to retaliate. Jane's account of her ordeal in the 'spare chamber' of the house, with its 'piled up mattresses and pillows' (4), is the tension of the real social distinction and the acute sense of the concrete manifestations of social rank (5). In this room Jane discovers what inequality means: 'I was a discord in Gateshead Hall, I was like nobody there'. (6)

T. Eagleton suggests that the realism in *Jane Eyre* contains an equal political ambivalence. (7) This may be true, however Charlotte Brontë shows us that it is possible for a woman to become a finer person, regardless of rank or status, because of her courage in facing difficulties. *Jane Eyre* is the story of a plain girl, alone in the world and dependent upon neither her relatives nor her friends, and she takes complete control of her own life. Jane's progress to freedom is the action of a modern woman. Her struggles and her troubles are her own, she seeks none to help her.

The lack of equality and truth that is structured in the novel is indicative of the scorn that was aimed at women, particularly gentlewomen. The status given to these women was on a par to a non-entity. Jane rebels against the inhuman cruelty she was subjected to. She is without love, affection, or companionship. This breeds a frustration within her soul which increases every time the Reeds taunt her. Charlotte Brontë invited the reader to share Jane's pain and shows her wrongfully accused of deceit: 'people think you are a good woman, but you are bad, hard-hearted. You are deceitful!' (8)

At Lowood, Jane is aware of the rejection she suffers from the only home she has ever known. Her rebellious streak is still very strong as she settles in at the school. The authority of Lowood is Brocklehurst, who runs the school with unfeeling rigidity and severe frugality. He rules the girls in his charge with imperious disdain, full of cant and hypocrisy. He claims 'his mission is to mortify in these girls the lusts of the flesh, to teach them to clothe themselves with shame-facedness.' (9) It could be considered no small irony that while Jane seeks her true identity and nature,

Brocklehurst insists 'that his substitute is conformity to convention of self-denial that is riddled with hypocrisy.' (10)

Such a realistic portrayal of the way girls and young women were treated in the nineteenth century shows the directness and passion of Charlotte Brontë's style, which throws open a strict and hypocritical society to full public scrutiny. Jane, in turn, must face new truths about herself and this new authority. This is when Brocklehurst forces Jane to face him. The tension mounts as Jane realises, 'of my own accord I could not have stirred, I was paralysed.' (11) Jane has to face the damage her Aunt Reed has inflicted on her. Branded a liar in the past, she is humiliated and suffers 'a deep grief' (12). The psychological realism of this part of the novel illustrates the growth and progress of Jane. The affection shown to her by Miss Temple makes her exclaim, 'I would not now have exchanged Lowood, for all its privations, for Gateshead and its daily luxuries.' (13)

Jane's development during her time at Lowood is indicative of Charlotte Brontë's realistic manner. Jane becomes a realistic character. Trollope wrote, 'the realism in art – by which we mean that which shall seem to be real – is different from "true life" and lies somewhere between naturalism and complete artificiality.' (14) This realism is evident when Jane desires liberty after Miss Temple marries. Charlotte Brontë wrote *Jane Eyre* in the first person, thus allowing the reader to share the restlessness which Jane suffers. She was attacked for this in *The Quarterly*, which accused her of bad taste and immorality: the story was so convincing that many were afraid of the truths which the novel articulated. A young woman who has no family, no home and no money should not become restless or desire excitement, since that was thought improper. Charlotte Brontë's realism was a challenge to contemporary morality.

Jane's acceptance of the post of governess at Thornfield is structurally very important. Her emotions, normally in turmoil, settle down, and she begins to enjoy contentment. Her dignified position gives her new confidence, although she still feels 'the restlessness in my nature.' (15) Everything changes as the world of romantic fiction, in the form of Rochester, obtrudes: the Byronic hero, unconventional in manner and looks. Jane's rebellious nature, which had raged against the Reeds and Brocklehurst, settles into the past. Her self-esteem grows, she no longer questions her position, and willingly acknowledges Rochester as her master.(16)

Rochester, who conceals a tragic secret, is repeatedly described as unattractive, but his 'dark face with stern features and a heavy brow' (17) does not deter Jane, because he treats her as an equal and encourages her to express her true feelings. She comes to love him for apparently very simple reasons: 'My help had been needed and claimed, I had given it.' (18) Rochester's tragedy is Jane's freedom, although it is a freedom found in outward submission. Romance begins to highlight the difference between sexual love and mere affection: 'I did not think I should tremble in this way,' says Jane of wakening emotions which are as real as Rochester's formerly jaded emotions are real, reawakened truthfully in his desire to possess and marry Jane. (19) Charlotte Brontë's realistic view of such feelings was again controversial, since women in the Victorian age were not supposed to enjoy sexual activity nor declare openly sexual feelings – the romantic element in the novel turns out to be surprisingly realistic, since Jane is a real, living being who will not deny her true nature.

The discovery of Rochester's mad wife causes Jane to go nearly half mad herself, although conscious reasoning drives her to seek another home. There, at Moorend, Jane has to struggle between the dictates of reason and the prompting of instinct. This conflict is brought to a climax when she clashes with the pious St John Rivers. St John is not a passionate man, and argues that it is Jane's duty to marry him; she is almost persuaded when she realises that to become his partner she must become a part of him, 'forced to keep the fire of my nature continually low.' (20) Jane's growing awareness of her own maturity forces her to see her life and the direction it was taking in a fresh light. St John Rivers would dominate Jane, and she would submit to him as she did to John Reed and Mr Brocklehurst. The figures of authority which caused Jane so much sorrow determined that she would not be dominated again.

The above scenes pass so quickly that Jane seems to grow in front of the reader's eyes. She confidently seeks out Rochester. Pauline Nester suggests that Jane and Rochester have a natural sympathy and mutual kinship which gives them a certain kind of equality. David Lodge agrees with this assertion, portraying Rochester as the kindred spirit to Jane, passionate, vital and above all unconventional. (21) But I disagree. Jane is innocent, and Rochester has abused her innocence through his secrecy. Their relationship cannot be equal. (22) Rochester claims Jane will be his, and Jane dreams of 'conversation and company forever' – he becomes very possessive, and in doing so releases her restraint so that she too becomes possessive. If Rochester had had real faith in Jane he would have told her everything from the start. Continually, Jane has to cope with other people imposing identities on her that she does not want, and Rochester is no exception.

Jane marries Rochester and we presume that they live happily ever after, but is she? The ending is so out of key with the rest of the novel that Eagleton writes, 'The heroine's lonely self-reproval is replaced by a glad submission to the censorings of a soul-mate. The figures are unequal, the 'lower' character (who is always the protagonist) can find in the 'higher' both an emulable image of achievement and an agreeable reflection of his or her own deviant individualism.' (23) Jane, who rebelled against John Reed and Mr Brocklehurst, does not rebel against Rochester. Thornfield appears to be the end of Jane's progress. Romance stirs within her and she ceases to question her position. Jane willingly calls her husband 'master'.

Ruskin is quoted as saying, 'Man is the door, the creator, the discoverer, while woman's intellect is not for creation or invention.' (24) Charlotte Brontë herself experienced the precarious line Victorian women were forced to walk of poverty, self-suppression along with injustice. Her realistic attempts to expose this male dominance in her novels enabled her to establish her own identity.

—2—

QUESTION: Discuss the portrayal of conflict between the sexes in *A Midsummer Night's Dream*

'The man shall have his mare again and all shall be well', says Puck in the middle of the play (1), and by the end of Act IV all is indeed well; Jack has got Jill and Shakespeare has the two pairs of runaway lovers about to be happily married at the same time as Theseus and Hippolyta, while Oberon and Titania dance now that they are 'new in amity' (2). And why not? *A Midsummer Night's Dream* is, after all, a comedy. However, the sexual conflict which appears in the play does seem to 'raise the possibility', as David Marshall puts it, that the play is 'not one of Shakespeare's happiest comedies.' (3)

Scene One introduces themes of male conquest over women, male rulership and female obedience, and these will cause all of the sexual conflict that happens in the play. However, Scene One could be interpreted in different ways; it could be portrayed as festive or tense. (4) The first speeches by Theseus and Hippolyta could be interpreted as them being impatient, looking forward to their wedding day, but it is Theseus's second speech which seems to bring in an undercurrent of tension between them:

> *Hippolyta, I wooed thee with my sword*
> *And won thy love doing thee injuries.* (5)

In the light of this image of male conquest over women, another evaluation of Hippolyta's speech is required, as she only speaks once in this scene and is not heard again until Act IV, and then there can be seen an element of disharmony; Hippolyta appears to be at odds with Theseus. David Marshall suggests that Hippolyta speaks with 'reason, dignity and diplomacy – as appropriate for a Queenly prisoner-of-war.' (6) The use of the word 'solemnities' to describe the marriage suggests the seriousness and gravity of the wedding day and not the joy there should perhaps be. Theseus continues in his second speech by saying that he will

> *wed [Hippolyta] in another key:*
> *With pomp, with triumph, and with revelling.* (7)

This could be Theseus trying to put the 'spirit of mirth' into the wedding, (8) but the words pomp, triumph and revelling 'sound as much like a military celebration as a wedding,' (9) ironic as this man won Hippolyta's love in combat. The opening of the play could therefore be seen as 'the evolution of order between the sexes,' (10) which develops throughout the play, and in which all the women are, or come to be, subordinate to the men.

In the next part of the first scene, Hippolyta is still present according to the stage directions, but Shakespeare gives her nothing to say. What is the meaning of her silence here? It seems strange that she should say nothing after hearing of Hermia's situation, and it is left to the director and actress to decide just how this silent presence should be portrayed. If Theseus's view is to be taken, it could be argued that Hippolyta remains silent out of loving respect, but this diminishes the tension between them. There is, furthermore, the suggestion that she is unhappy when Theseus asks her, 'What cheer, my love?' (11), which goes some way to enforcing our sense of conflict between them. It is interesting to note that in the BBC production of the play, the director both avoided the problem of Hippolyta's silence and accounted for sexual conflict in a single gesture: Theseus left her to discuss Egeus and Hermia's business in another room. It appears, then, that Shakespeare, by giving Hippolyta nothing to say, is enforcing the male dominance in the play, and Hippolyta's silence could be seen to speak very loud in portraying conflict.

When in Act IV Hippolyta speaks again there is more evidence of the tension between the two: Hippolyta, while relating the story of when she was hunting with Hercules and Cadmus, appears to be challenging Theseus's masculinity, and perhaps even his right to dominate over her. Theseus tries to convince Hippolyta that his hounds, which are 'bred out of the Spartan kind', are equal to those of Hercules and Cadmus (12); 'Judge when you hear', he states, but again Shakespeare does not let it be known what she thinks. (13)

Perhaps the most obvious sexual conflict in Act One is the dispute Hermia has with her father, Egeus, about marriage. Egeus demands obedience from Hermia and begs 'the ancient privilege of Athens' that 'as she is mine, I may dispose of her' (14); Hermia is faced with either marriage to her father's choice, or with death. In contrast to Hippolyta, Hermia does speak her mind over his and will not relent:

> *So will I grow, so live, so die, my lord,*
> *Ere I will yield my virgin patent up*
> *Unto his lordship whose unwished yoke*
> *My soul consents not to give sovereignty. (15)*

Hippolyta, it appears, had no choice but to have her 'sovereignty' taken away from her, but Hermia does not want to relinquish her independence. This shows Hermia to be headstrong, and emphasises that it is only herself and Lysander who are really in love. Yet because of the patriarchal ideology of the play Egeus is shown to want to keep his dominance over his daughter. Egeus's reasons appear to be economic ones, he insists that Hermia is 'private property' (16), that

> *she is mine and all my right of her*
> *I do estate unto Demetrius. (17)*

The word 'estate' is especially significant here: the marriage is a kind of deal. Egeus is backed up by Theseus, who wants to be seen as the man of law and order in Athens, and who also shows his view of what he thinks women should be by saying that if Hermia were to go to a nunnery she would live all her life

> *a barren sister....*
> *Chanting faint hymns to the cold, fruitless moon. (18)*

Her life, the argument goes, will be wasted if she does not produce 'fruit', or children. Duke Theseus seems to want everyone to married off, whether they like it or not, to keep things nicely in order.

In the fairy world of the woods there are parallels with the world of Athens, as the theme of male dominance is carried on by Oberon because Titania is 'in rebellion against Oberon's authority.' (19) It is here again that Shakespeare observes conflict between the sexes. Oberon can be seen, like Theseus, to be trying to establish order.

Shakespeare shows conflict between Helena and Demetrius, but this time in reverse from what has been seen already: Helena cannot get Demetrius to love her again, even though she sinks so low as to say, 'I am your spaniel' (20) and 'the more you beat me I will fawn on you' (21), but here it seems that Demetrius has the right to refuse, where Hippolyta and Hermia did not. James Calderwood argues that when Helena says

> *Your wrongs do set a scandal on my sex*
> *We cannot fight for love, as men do.*
> *We should be woo'd and were not made to woo (22),*

Oberon observes a possible inversion of sexual roles and sets about restoring order. But this, of course, leads to more confusion and conflict between the pairs of lovers, which in turn has to be resolved.

Oberon's own conflict with Titania is over the Indian boy whom she refuses to give to him. Is Shakespeare portraying this conflict because he believes that the boy should be in Oberon's masculine world and become a 'knight of his train'? (23) In Act Two, the determined Titania defends her right to the boy on the grounds of friendship with his mother:

> *And for her sake do I rear up the boy;*
> *And for her sake will not part with him. (24)*

However, by Act Four – albeit under the influence of 'love in idleness – when asked again by Oberon to surrender the boy, she instantly agrees. Having got what he wanted, Oberon states,

> *And now I have the boy I will undo*
> *This hateful imperfection of her eyes. (25)*

But instead of anger at being tricked, Titania appears to have forgotten everything. The conflict which Shakespeare so carefully set up at the beginning of the play is allowed to disappear abruptly, apparently in the interests of achieving a happy closure to the play.

A Midsummer Night's Dream certainly seems to project an ideology which is hostile to women. This is bound to affect our view of the play as a celebration of marriage. A quotation from Goethe's *Elective Affinities* used by David Marshall seems appropriate here:

> *In a comedy we see marriage as an ultimate goal, reached only after*
> *surmounting obstacles which fill several acts; and at the moment the goal is*
> *achieved, the curtain falls and a momentary satisfaction warms our hearts.*
> *(26)*

However, the way Shakespeare develops his themes of male dominance and female subordination suggests problems which such an ending like the one to *A Midsummer Night's Dream* can't really tidy away. Some of the disputes and conflicts would not be out of place in a tragedy, and perhaps sentiments like this are echoed in the mechanicals' play of Pyramus and Thisbe, that 'most lamentable comedy' (27), a contradictory description which seems true of *A Midsummer Night's Dream* itself.

—3—

QUESTION: Some critics find Shelley's poetry eloquently prophetic, while others view it as verbal vapour. Basing your response on a close analysis of a representative selection of his poems, discuss why you think these opposing views have developed and determine how far each is justifiable.

Percy B. Shelley was an idealist, he believed everyone should love freely and naturally. However, he believed in his own ideals, so his work was not appreciated by a society scaling a ladder towards materialism and industrialisation. Shelley was influenced by Godwin and later turned to the philosophy of Plato. The ideas of Plato were seeds of a creation 'lying burningly on the divine hand'. In the fifth century BC Plato considered the paradoxical relations between pleasure and pain. Love begins with a wave of euphoria, but all too soon it becomes painful. Shelley's love for the world was painful to him, and his writings were a channel for the emotions and sensations he felt within himself.

Because of his philosophy, many people thought he was mad. While daily experience shaped other poets' thoughts, to Shelley they meant very little. He was a solitary intellect and his ideas came from his own mental processes, from his studies and from his visions of the future or his dreams of the past. He lacked the ability to see the world and suffered for his isolation. He had the power to be able to argue his cause. His reactions to political, social and personal worlds are violent and are contained within his poetry. This caused many critics to criticise his work.

His powerful poem 'Queen Mab' was considered very powerful in working-class radical circles. The poem includes ideas from many philosophers such as Locke, Hume, Rousseau and Godwin. The radicals believed that their generation was beginning to get things right after centuries of mess and failure. In the poem, Ianthe is woken from her sleep by the fairy Mab and taken on a journey to have the past explained to her, what was miserable in the world, and how societies of the future could be better. The symbols of misery, unhappiness and crimes against humanity are a forbidding message in the poems:

> *Where Athens, Rome and Sparta stood,*
>   *there is a moral desert now.*
> *Where Cicero and Antoninus lived,*
>   *A cowled and hypocritical monk*
>   *Prays, curses and deceives. (1)*

The learning and love is barren and empty. The superstitions that religion holds over man, the cause of wars and death, is prominent throughout the poems. In the Old Testament, Kings ruled as God's right-hand men. They held the power of life and death over mortal man:

> *The King, the wearer of a gilded chain,*
> *That binds his soul to abjectness, the fool*
> *Whom courtiers nickname monarch, whilst a slave*
> *Even to the basest appetites. (2)*

This condemnation of monarchy suggests a reference to the French Revolution, and an accusation against the English monarch of neglecting his subjects. The myth might result in a reader describing the poem as 'verbal vapour'. The layers of the poem have to be interpreted. The evil Shelley exposes fails to explain why the history of the world was so depressing. The power within a man to love is also a power to drive a man to be devoted to a religion or a political body. Godwin believed that evil lies in 'institutions', in all the organs of authority that man has ever created.

Religion and the power of man are two items that possessed Shelley, he proclaimed himself to be an atheist, for all that he could believe was what he saw. Yet he repeatedly turned to mythology. Browning praised Shelley's poetry as a 'sublime fragmentary essay towards the presentment of the correspondency of the universe of Deitry, and of the natural to the spiritual and of the actual to the ideal.' (3)

Shelley tried to find the truth of what or who was God. In his search, he, like Blake, offered a vision of a last judgment that each man passes on himself, by his own assertion and in the cultivation of his own understanding. This vision of the last judgment is one of the most eloquently prophetic aspects of his work.

The force of evil must give way to good in the end. The suggestion is that nature is the overpowering good and that man is the source of destruction. This is symbolised in the line:

> *Blast the human flower even in its tenderest bud. (4)*

The rhetoric shows how man enjoys destruction and evil all in the name of the 'good of mankind':

> *War is the statesman's game,*
>   *the priest's delight,*
> *Those too the tyrant serve, who, skilled to snare*
> *The feet of justice in the toils of law*
>   *Stand ready to oppress the weaker still. (5)*

Shelley's poetry was composed within the self. This shows itself in the range of moods and emotions, and in the significant and profound experiences it has. However, the fears he confronts are contradicted in the 'Hymn to Intellectual Beauty'. He is shaken by the vast implications of his own mortality:

> *Why fear and dream and death and birth*
> *Cast on the day-light of this Earth*
> *Such gloom – and why man has such scope*
> *For love and hate, despondency and hope? (6)*

The conviction in this poem is Shelley's belief in the true conception of the power that belonged to man and nature. He wanted to confirm the immortality of man.

The Greek mythology Shelley used in 'Prometheus Unbound' could be another reason why many were critical of his work. 'In Mr Shelley's poetry', wrote one critic,

> *all is brilliance, vacuity and confusion. We are dazzled by the multitude of words which sound as if they denote something very grand or splendid...*
> *not a trace of it remains upon the memory. (7)*

This makes his poetry seem not eloquently prophetic, but verbal vapour, as if he was just using myths to sound impressive. But it may indicate the way religion was losing its authority over people, leaving poetry to take over. 'Prometheus Unbound' was a fight to save mankind from the clutches of oppression. The answer was in mankind's own hands. Hercules, who through strength and endurance performed many feats, and his last exploit was to kill the eagle that daily devoured Prometheus. Jupiter, who sent the eagle, was angry because the great friend of mankind stole fire from heaven and gave it to the sons of mankind. Jupiter made Prometheus's liver grow every night so that he would suffer continuous torture until Hercules slew the eagle and burst asunder the bonds that held prisoner the friend of man. Prometheus is a poem of fury and anger, prophetic in its belief that man must be freed from oppression.

If the despair of Prometheus is true, then man is certainly heading for disaster. Prometheus symbolises the spirit of humanity. He begs Earth to repeat the words with which he defied Jupiter:

> *Venerable Mother!*
> *All else who live and suffer take from thee*
> *Some comfort; flowers and fruits and happy sounds*
> *And love, though fleeting; these may not be mine.*
> *But mine own words, I pray, deny me not. (8)*

The agony of Prometheus is continuous, yet he can forgive, and in one act of graciousness has the dual capacity for joy.

The image of Earth and the hosts of heaven, spirits of time and eternity are embodied and vivified, to unite in the reign of love over the universe. The fate of Prometheus suggests that he was a celebration of the deliverance of the spirit of humanity from the iron grasp of its foes – the myth was in a way prophetic.

Jupiter is locked with Prometheus in a battle which is passionate in its intensity. In the cave of Demogorgon, Asia and Parthea, they question who is the creator of all the living world. Each question is answered, 'God, Almighty God, Merciful God'. When Asia asks who made

> *Terror, madness, crime, remorse,*
> *Which form the links of the great chain of things,*
> *To every thought within the mind of man*
> *Sway and drag heavily, and each one reels*
> *Under their load towards the pit of death, (9)*

Demogorgon replies, 'He reigns'. Prometheus, chained to a rock, suffers the torments of man, and asks, 'Can a merciful God who reigns be so cruel?' But Prometheus, unlike the God he condemns, has the ability to forgive. Mortals bend the knee to the unseen God, cowed by the threat of damnation.

Jupiter, the supreme being, is aware that mortal man knows that his time will come. Saturn, the figure of time, waits for no one, not even Jupiter, and in Act III Jupiter falls. Hercules rescues Prometheus and the powers of nature rejoice at his liberation. Power, imagination, love and nature reign, and in everyone there is shown to be the capacity for beauty and love. This again is a very prophetic element in Shelley's work.

Religion was the key to Shelley's earlier work. He wanted a new heaven and a new earth, as prophesied by the Bible. He wanted forgiveness so that mankind could begin again. Some critics feel that he was neither rebellious nor prophetic, just experimenting with myths and metaphors which justify the charge of 'verbal vapour', but what remains from his poetry is a strong feeling of love and pity for his fellow men, and a prophetic feeling for how their circumstances could be improved:

> *Me – who am as a nerve o'er which do creep,*
> *The else unfelt oppressions of this Earth. (10)*

—4—

QUESTION: Discuss Charlotte Brontë's treatment of the concept of control in *Villette*.

The notion of control is present in a variety of guises throughout *Villette*. There is the inner control of Lucy Snowe's confinement of her emotions and true nature, as well as the enforced, outward control of those who manipulate Lucy for their own ends. Through both of these Brontë highlights the control imposed upon women in a patriarchal society, the constraining effects of which she herself experienced. E. A. Knies observes that the novel charts Lucy's attempt to determine what her personality should be in a hostile world; (1) but the novel also concerns Brontë's own quest for an identity free not only from external control, but from the control Lucy herself has been taught to exert.

Lucy's own methods of self-control are demonstrated in her first introduction to the school-room. When the rebellious Dolores gets out of hand Lucy's reaction is simply to lock her away in the closet, so concealing what she cannot cope with. Such physical restraint is symbolic of the mental restraint which she also exhibits. As Willis observes, Lucy is emotionally starved, yet highly emotional.(2) Unsure of what to do with her emotions, she locks them away, so to speak, in what Tony Tanner calls her 'house of consciousness' (3):

> *pedigree, social position, and recondite intellectual acquisition, occupied about the same space and place in my interests and thoughts; they were my third-class lodgers – to whom could be assigned only the small sitting-room and the little back bedroom; even if the dining and drawing-rooms should be empty, I have never confessed it to them, as thinking minor accommodation better suited to their circumstances.(4)*

Lucy uses this image of a house to describe the state of her mind, as if excusing her odd priorities by natural disposition. Through the experiences of Paulina at Bretton, Lucy has observed the pain and rejection which come of emotional display and attachment, so she seeks to contain her emotions within the designated rooms of the safe house, hiding herself from the pain of emotional involvement by imprisoning her physical being in the houses she inhabits in both England and Villette. She is mentally constrained within physical constraint.

Her reserve, constraint and love of formality are sharply conveyed in the chapters concerning her time at Bretton, where, she admits, 'I liked peace so well, and sought stimulus so little.'(5) The 'large peaceful rooms' and the secure order of the 'well-arranged furniture' render her a reassuring image of what she supposes are her own needs;(6) she and her ardour are comfortably shut away with others whom she describes revealingly as 'inmates'.(7)

The security of this voluntary imprisonment does not last, however. Forced out into the world, she chooses to travel to the Continent, a decision which conveys the promise of liberty, but which leads simply to a further act of refuge as she takes up residence in the nursery 'watch-tower' (the better to look inwards?), keeping herself secure from the outside world behind the castle-like 'blank wall' of M. Beck's school.(8) Such confinement, however severe, turns out to be inadequate to Lucy's need to hide. Attracted by its 'seclusion', 'gloom', (9) and finding it a place where she can 'studiously hold the quick of [her] nature' (10), Lucy retreats to the alley within the enclosure of the school's grounds. The alley is suggestive in other ways: Lucy's mind is not only confined, but, of course, 'straight and narrow', just as repressed as the 'tintless flowers' she finds in the garden.(11) Once again, moreover, her attempt to find solace in her surroundings drives her deeper into self-constraint: she finds only the emblems of her own repression. Just as Graham gives her the kind of attention one would to 'unobtrusive articles of furniture', so she strives to become more of a 'neutral, passive thing.' (12)

However, the exhibitionist society of Villette – voyeuristic, theatrical, and, in its Catholicism, confessional – makes such self-concealment ever more difficult to sustain. Lucy begins to venture out into the world induced by Beck's tantalising question, 'Will you go backward or forward?' (13) Lucy admits that, 'left to myself, I should infallibly have let this chance slip.'(14); nonetheless, she is unable to resist Beck's provocation and rises to the challenge, endeavouring to overcome her fear of the trials that lie ahead. Despite being 'tremulous from head to foot' (15), Lucy takes her step into the classroom, adding to her confined world another room. Knies contends that part of her nature is now fulfilled: she is no longer 'lying the stagnant prey of mould and rust' but is polishing her faculties and 'whetting them to a keen edge with constant use.' (16) This is, perhaps, a shade optimistic on Knies's part. The classroom is just another room, and Lucy's powers of affection remain repressed. Convincing herself that she is 'loverless and inexpectant of love'(17) – the unusual word 'inexpectant' may convey a repressed desire for motherhood – Lucy has no one to induce a release of her self-enforced, self-protecting control. Her passions remain concealed within the safe house of her mind.

Life with the Brettons entails, however, a real broadening of Lucy's emotional experience, prompting feelings from her of both attraction and repulsion. The long, highly-charged description of Lucy watching Vashti conveys how Lucy's emotional state is persistently linked to her environment – here, the glittering vulgarity of high society, like the yearnings it awakens, draws and repels her in the same instant:

> *It was a marvellous sight: a mighty revelation. It was a spectacle low,*
> *horrible, immoral. (18)*

She finds this brief lapse of control over her emotions so overwhelming that she demands of herself, 'Thus far and no further!' (19) as her passions seem to reach a peak in the spontaneous combustion of the theatre. A similar scene occurs when Lucy momentarily lets her self-control slip when she is forced to act in a play. She enjoys the rush of emotion involved, but finds it frightening and resolves again to enforce control over herself. On being asked to dance she tells the reader, 'I had acted enough for one evening; it was time I retired into myself and my ordinary life.' (20) Acting seems to her, as it does for Fanny Price in Austen's *Mansfield Park*, an immoral sport, necessary to society but destructive to individual integrity, for displaying herself and her emotion in the play means becoming part of society, throwing open the windows of her passions to public (and her own) scrutiny. In this respect, Knies's belief that the novel charts Lucy's attempt to find a personality in a hostile world seems simplistic, since the same world has made Lucy partly hostile to herself: it is her own restraint she has to combat as well as that of 'the world'.

The play sequence of the novel repays further investigation, since it is here that the drama of individual need and social control is most prominent. Lucy is compelled not only to play another; she does it for the pleasure of others. Her 'character' in the play is not her own character, but she defends it as if it were; the social role is one which she feels she must own: 'nobody must meddle; the things must not be forced upon me. Just let me dress myself.' (21) She clings to her own regular clothing rather than allow herself to be submerged totally in the costume intended for her, accepting some items from M.Paul and declining others. Through this symbolism of clothing vs. costume, Brontë conveys Lucy's resisting compliance not only with society, but with the world of men; she allows her individuality to be impinged on only partially by the male. The play therefore turns out to be of paradoxical benefit to Lucy, allowing her to act out the demands of male–female relationships and to perform her insistence on reaching a compromise with the impositions of a controlling, male social world.

The play sequence is in a sense a model for the way Lucy copes with the cameo world of Villette itself. She finds that she cannot fit any of the male-defined roles laid down for her: she is not the submissive future wife (Paulina), nor the perfect matriarch (Mrs Bretton), nor the flirtatious object of male desire (Ginevra). Lucy's rejection of these roles causes consternation, prompting Ginevra to demand, 'Who are you, Miss Lucy Snowe?' Lucy's value is shown to lie in her being non-typical, if non-ideal in the social sense. Lucy becomes, as Kate Millett observes, Ginevra's greatest challenge.(22) Failing to understand Lucy's detachment from social norms, she uses her beauty to provoke Lucy and win her admiration. This is not to imply, however, as Millett does, that Lucy has a 'masculine lust' for Ginevra,(23) nor, as some other critics do, that there is latent lesbian feeling between them (24); rather, that Ginevra's advance shows society attempting to encompass Lucy in an image of 'feminine' compliance, and failing, just as Paul's attempts to encompass her have failed.

Nonetheless, it is Paul's affection and understanding which eventually draw her out.(25) The school house with which he provides her allows her independence and a medium throught which to express a character newly nurtured. The mansion of the inner self is turned outwards in a healthier, physical manifestation. No longer merely a looker-on from the watch-tower, she can take on a positive role defined largely by herself and, eventually, controlled by no one. There is, as Gilbert and Gubar remark, no attic in this house where Lucy can be locked away or, still more important, lock herself away. In occupying the whole of this attic-free house, she declares her freedom from outward control and from its inner representation, her own oppressive self-control. There is, however, a snag in this interpretation. Lucy's 'entire' occupation of the house depends on Paul's absence, and it is Paul's shipwreck which guarantees it. To be free, it seems, Lucy must be alone. Therefore, while Norman Sherry states, rather surprisingly, that the final relationship of Lucy and Paul is the traditional one for Brontë, with the man as kindly master, (26) one might argue that in *Villette* Brontë has moved beyond this 'traditional' ending to the belief not in man's superiority within marriage, but in the impossibility of egalitarian relationships in a society dominated by male values.

The final paradox of the concept of control in Villette is Brontë's way of showing that attempts to control Lucy very often have the opposite effect. M. Beck's endeavouring to keep Lucy from Paul by drugging her in fact frees her from physical and mental restraint. She effortlessly frees herself from the confines of the safe house of her mind as the doors 'yield to [her] hand... with propitious facility.' (27) Freedom comes from restraint itself, from the rebellion which it induces, and opium gives to Lucy a new freedom of imagination, beyond the reach of the reason which, throughout the novel exemplifies her self-control:

> *then, just at that moment, the doors of my heart would shake, bolt and bar*
> *would yield, reason would leap in, vigorous and revengeful.(28)*

In her drug-induced state, imagination can triumph, 'impetuous and venturous.'(29) The liberating force of imagination was no less important to Brontë herself, for it was imagination which allowed her to write and so reach beyond the limited opportunities available to women of her class and situation. Both Brontë and Lucy therefore escape control, the one through her writing, the other through what Tony Tanner calls 'an expanded consciousness'(30) as Lucy progresses from the 'clean' and 'ancient' classicism of Bretton to the improvised, unpredictable Gothicism of the park at *Villette*:

> *a land of enchantment... a region, not of trees and shadow, but of the*
> *strangest architectural wealth – of altar and of temple, of pyramid, obelisk*
> *and sphynx.*

This is landscape where reason and centralised control have been banished and where the imagination can rove freely.

Villette, then, both explores and exposes the control which society inflicts on the individual, and the way in which the individual may absorb such control within herself. Brontë demonstrates the ideologies which support this control, most prominently the constraining and painfully unfulfillable view of the ideal woman. Moreover, she challenges these dominant views as she presents in Lucy Snowe a figure who refuses to succumb to pre-conceived images of female value.

Exercises

In this section we will look at different aspects of the essays you have just been reading:

- Introductions
- Paragraphing
- Use of critical sources
- Use of quotations from the primary text
- Conclusions
- Answering the question

Introductions

1. Compare the introductions of essays 3 and 4. Which of the following is true of which introduction?

   (i) distinguishes between different aspects of the subject
   (ii) excludes information which the marker is bound to know already
   (iii) leads us forward into the second paragraph
   (iv) shows how the question is relevant to the text
   (v) gets the reader interested
   (vi) unfolds so that one sentence connects clearly with the next

2. Obviously one of these essays has the better introduction! You should aim to do all of the above when you begin an essay, although you don't have to do it exactly as above. Compare, for example, the introductions of essays 2 and 4. What differences can you find?

3. You might find that introduction 2 works better for you – it's snappy, gets you into the subject without fuss, and prevents you from waffling away for a page with definitions taken from a dictionary. In particular, introduction 2 might provide a good model for when you have to do a timed answer. There are pitfalls, however. Can you think of some?

4. The language of introduction 4 is well-suited to its style and purpose. Look at the chain of words used to *discriminate* between aspects of the subject: 'There is... as well as... Through both of these... Knies observes... but the novel also concerns...'.

Can you find instances of this kind of language in any of the other introductions?

5. Essays 1 and 2 both employ the word 'However' in their introductions. Why?

⚠ *Don't be remotely tempted to write an introduction like the one in essay 3! Piling on the background detail for its own sake is a waste of your time and the marker's.*

6. Look again at the introduction to essay 4. You will see that it follows a clear structure, with each sentence contributing something distinctive. Look at how the student has followed this order of functions:

    (i)   enumerate different aspects of the question
    (ii) explain one aspect of the question
    (iii) explain other aspect of the question
    (iv) state wider purpose of both of these aspects
    (v)   quote critical example of simplistic approach
    (vi) show how your own approach is more sophisticated
    (vii) focus on main theme of essay

    You will see that some of the functions are contained within a single, elaborate sentence. Not all good introductions look like this, but use this example as a model to get you going. Now try to re-write the introduction to essay 2 so that it conforms to this pattern.

Paragraphing

A good introduction, we have seen, makes it clear immediately that different aspects of the question have been grasped. Good paragraphing will show that those aspects are being explored in an orderly and discriminating way.

1. Compare the ways in which essays 3 and 4 begin their paragraphs. What differences do you observe?

2. The opening sentences of the paragraphs in essay 4 use words that indicate the relationship between the points made in the new paragraph and the old (our old friend 'however', for example). What are some of the others?

3. You've just looked for words that 'indicate the relationship' between paragraphs. This sense of inter-relationship is vital for a really successful essay. When you plan, you need to think of the different aspects of the question, but also of the relationship between those aspects. Here are some examples of functional relationships between paragraphs. Try to match them against what you've found in essays 2 and 4 in particular (you may find that some paragraphs combine two or more of the functions identified):

   (i)   underlines by giving further evidence
   (ii) indicates a further aspect of a topic already treated
   (iii) qualifies a former point by reference to another part of the text
   (iv) highlights a part of the text that is unusual in relation to the question
   (v)   establishes a parallel with a point already made

   ⚠ *Whatever the relationship, it should be dynamic and reflective: if you begin every paragraph with 'also', 'another example', or 'in addition', you will give the impression of not having really thought about the question.*

4 With dynamism and reflection go relevance. Good paragraphing never leaves you in doubt as to where you stand in relation to the question which has been asked. You may have noticed that essay 3 strains towards relevance by throwing in the key terms from the question every now and then. What is the difference between this and the way adopted by the other essays?

5. We know from the Core Elements that good paragraphs work because they have a structure: different sentences have different jobs to perform, and they do so in an orderly way. Here is a list of typical sentence functions in the paragraphs of an English essay. Look through essay 4 again and see if you can spot examples of them:

   (i)   identify the topic of the paragraph
   (ii) quote details of paragraph topic from primary text
   (iii) quote critical material related to topic
   (iv) refer to another primary text with a similar topic
   (v)   seek contradiction within paragraph topic
   (vi) summarise/re-phrase/revise paragraph topic.

Now look at essay 3 and see how you could improve the structure of any of its paragraphs.

6. Some of the paragraphs in essay 4 follow the functions given on the previous page in the order listed. Now try to write your own paragraph, based on a text you're familiar with and using the six functions identified, in their stated order.

7. Remember that not all paragraphs will have the same structure, but all of them should display a majority of the functions you have just been practising. Choose another paragraph from essay 4 and work out how it is structured. What functions are the different sentences performing?

Use of critical sources

One of the major differences between degree level and A-level work is that you have to show knowledge of critical controversy surrounding the texts you're writing about. This is not to blunt your own responses to the texts, but to sharpen them up, to show that you can account for other points of view in developing your own approach to the topic. Remember that you have to record critical citations properly, as set out in Core Element 6.

1. What do you notice about the way critical sources are used by the authors of the four essays?

2. Like paragraphing, critical citation should be dynamic, an occasion for saying something more. It follows that you should aim to say something about the words you are quoting, and not simply quote because you feel in need of moral support. You could, for example:

   (i) disagree outright (it's often a good idea to quote someone you don't agree with so that you can show that you're thinking!)

  (ii) partially agree

 (iii) choose one particular word or phrase which seems apt or wrong, and explain why

 (iv) explain why the opinion cited is useful as an interpretative tool

  (v) identify or question the assumptions behind the opinion

Can you find any instances of such manoeuvres in the four essays? Can you locate moments where the student might beneficially have adopted one such manoeuvre but didn't?

3. It's very important to use the right language to signal your relationship to quoted criticism: as in life in general, you don't want to be too brusque or too reticent. Look at essay 4 and make a note of the words and phrases that are used to signal the functions you have identified above.

Use of quotations from primary texts

It is always important to show that what you have to say bears some relation to the texts in question. Quoting from those texts is, therefore, another way of maintaining relevance, but you have to be careful: in essay 3, for instance, the quotations from Shelley sometimes have only a marginal relationship, if any, to the way they have been introduced. Just quoting is nothing like enough: the quotations must cohere with the argument you are advancing.

1. There are two kinds of quotations from primary texts: *illustrative* and *exploratory*. With an illustrative quotation, you don't say anything about the quotation beyond the point you have used to introduce it. With an exploratory quotation, you say something extra afterwards, perhaps about some detail of the quotation (a word or phrase, an assumption), which allows you to make an additional and possibly unexpected point – one that deepens or qualifies the point you used to introduce it. All good essays achieve a balance between these two kinds of quotation. Look through the four essays and see if you can distinguish between instances of the two types.

2. Now consider the exploratory quotations more carefully. What different kinds of things did the students have to say about the passages they were quoting? Are there any words or phrases that are useful in saying such things?

> ⚠️ *A golden rule with quotation from primary texts: If you are going to quote a long passage, you must say quite a lot about the quotation in order to justify its inclusion. It follows that illustrative quotations will generally be short, while exploratory quotations may (although not necessarily) be more extensive.*

71

Conclusions

We've already looked briefly at conclusions in the Core Elements Section (pp.26–7). Have another look at what you found out there and see if you can apply it to the endings of the essays printed in this section.

1. Which seems to you the most successful conclusion of the four, and why?

2. How could any of the four conclusions have been improved?

3. Three of the essays make use of a quotation in the concluding paragraph which may be taken from a source other than the primary text under discussion. This is very common in English essays and articles. Why? What are the advantages of doing this?

4. None of the four conclusions uses the kind of vocabulary you might expect: 'In conclusion', 'finally', etc. What means do they use instead to signify an ending?

Answering the question

You've already come to some judgment about how well each of the essays answers the question set. There are, as you may have noticed, different kinds of question.

1. Look at the four essay questions. Which of them would you say match the following categories?

    (i)   consider examples of a given concept in the text
    (ii) consider validity of a statement about the text
    (iii) consider validity of contrasting statements about the text
    (iv) consider relationship between a text and a remark not explicitly pertaining to it.
    (v)   consider validity of a statement in relation to specified aspects of the text

2. You should have noticed that the two best essays respond to a question of type (i) above. This does not mean that 'Discuss role of concept *x*' questions are easier! In fact, there are all sorts of dangers in answering such questions: there is, for example, no argument to start from, so that you either invent one for yourself

(a challenge) or fall into the trap of simply reciting instances of the concept as you find them in the text ('another example of *x*..., a further example of *x*..., yet another example of *x*'). Have a look at essays 2 and 4, especially the introductions and paragraph openings, and see how they overcome this danger. How do they go about 'inventing an argument' while remaining relevant to the question which has been asked?

3. Although questions of types 1(iii), 1(iv) and 1(v) have their own demands, they are all variants of 1(ii), so much of what is true of type 1(ii) will be relevant to the other types. The first step with a 'statement about the text' question is, obviously, to work out what exactly the statement is saying. This may not be as easy as it sounds. There are three basic procedures that you should follow, in this order:

   (i) Consider carefully the key words in the question, what they mean, and what implications they have – the key words will direct you towards the broad areas you need to cover.

   (ii) Consider the statement as a whole – remember that a claim is being made about the text, so you have to understand not only the key terms but the relationships between them. In order to do this, you could try re-phrasing the claim in several different ways so that you're completely happy with it.

   (iii) Remember that the claim is being made so that you can explore and dispute it. It isn't there to be swallowed whole or discarded. Aim to divide your time between running with the claim (thinking about why it's interesting or useful) and evaluating it.

Look at the following example of someone engaging with the key words and claim from the question answered by essay 1:

It has been suggested that in *Jane Eyre* Charlotte Brontë aims at a 'union of realism and romance' (King). Examine the structure and meaning of the novel in the light of this claim.

---

key words in quotation: union, realism, romance

key words in question: structure, meaning

realism: naturalistic portrayal of the outer and inner world, true to life, accepting disappointment, frustration.

romance: unreal, idealistic solutions to unhappiness; happy marriages; rambling stories of people looking for something.
union: bringing together; implies that realism and romance are different, conflicting things and need to be brought together. Can the union work?'

'aims' also a key word! Does Brontë succeed? Is this what is being aimed at, or are there other important structural features? Is it appropriate to consider intentions in this way?

structure: development of the novel, the way it is put together; parallel or contrasting scenes.

meaning: how to interpret what happens, mostly to Jane: what is the meaning of her experiences?

claim: the structure of the novel, and the development of Jane as a character, show different elements – romantic ones and realistic ones; where is the conflict between them and is it resolved?

Using this example as a model, try to break down the question for essay 3 (you should be able to do this even without any knowledge of Shelley!):

Some critics find Shelley's poetry eloquently prophetic, while others view it as verbal vapour. Basing your response on a close analysis of a representative selection of his poems, discuss why you think these opposing views have developed and determine how far each is justifiable.

4. Now look again at essay 3 and work out how it could have been improved.

⚠ *It can often be useful to find out about the source of the quotation; ask your tutor where it comes from so that you can research its background and find out more about the argument being proposed. Concentrate on the argument, not the author of the quotation – this is not an opportunity for making generalised statements about the person who proposed the idea.*

5. The exercises you have been doing apply to all kinds of 'statement questions'. With these exercises in mind, can you think of anything you should look out for in particular when dealing with types 1(iii), 1(iv), and 1(v) (p.72)?

Summary: a procedure to follow

So far we've been looking at different aspects of English essays. What is needed now is to pull everything together in the form of a procedure that you can follow every time you write an essay in English Studies. Try the following:

1. Break down the question, making sure that you understand all of it. When there is a selection of questions, don't choose one immediately without thinking critically about the others; it might turn out to be more difficult!

2. List all the different topics the question is asking you to consider.

3. List the parts of the text(s) that are relevant to those topics. Be selective, since your choice of evidence may influence the structure you adopt. With strongly narrative texts (most novels and plays) it is inevitable that your choice of episodes or passages will sometimes follow the course of 'events', but you must choose carefully, with an awareness of how a given event relates to others in the text. When you are planning an essay about poetry, don't simply aim to write a paragraph on one poem, then the next on another, and so on – think about how they are related, how one poem may correspond to several different aspects of your argument.

4. Sort out where the points of controversy are. This means doing some critical reading. Find some critical quotations you would endorse, and some you think you might want to qualify or contradict. Use material taken in note form from lectures and seminars.

5. Put the information you now have into some sort of plan. Refer back to the Paragraphing section (p.68) that you've just done and sort out the relationships between the different points you have on your list. Remember that you must show an awareness of the different views that could be taken of the topic or claim. It might be helpful to explain the plan to a friend at this stage – often a good way of finding out whether it all sounds logical.

6. Think about what sort of introduction you will write. How can you best lead the reader in to the different aspects of the question you are going to consider? Look again at the Introductions section (p.67) you have just completed.

7. Get writing! It may be that as you go along, and especially when you consider the details of quotations, you will want to deviate from some aspect of your plan. Don't be afraid of doing this (a really good essay will always give the air of spontaneous thought), but keep checking against your plan to make sure that you're on the right track. Make sure you structure your paragraphs properly. If you get stuck, use the Paragraphing section (pp.68–70) you have just worked through to show you what kind of job your next sentence might have to do.

8. Think about the sort of conclusion you want to write; look again at the endings of the sample essays and see what you can do.

9. Make sure you have referenced the essay fully, in accordance with the guidelines set out in Core Element 6, pp.38–45.

10. Proofread! Nothing irritates a marker more than careless errors. Try reading the essay out loud to see if it sounds right.

Essays in History

Sample Essays

What follows is a sample of essays submitted by first-year students of History over the past year. There are three essays, on different subjects, and each one gained a different pass mark, A, B or C. Satisfy yourself that you're familiar with the Marking Criteria section of this book (pp.49–51) and then read through all the essays, trying to decide which essay gained which mark. You might like to make a note of any passages that fulfil particular aspects of the criteria, or which seem to you especially successful or unsuccessful for any other reasons. Think, for example, about how well each essay answers the question set. After the essays, there are some exercises for you to look at.

> ⚠ *No end-notes are included in these samples, although the numbers are given in the body of each piece. Never neglect referencing in your own work!*

—1—

QUESTION: Account for the longevity of Sir Robert Walpole's political ascendancy.

Sir Robert Walpole is often considered to be Britain's first prime minister (1). Not only did he see a period of stability in British politics, but he also maintained the longest period as premier. But why was this? What are the reasons behind such a lengthy term in office? This essay will attempt to answer these questions by looking at perhaps the three major aspects of Walpole's term: the demise of the Tories as a political force; Walpole's political abilities; and his financial skills.

1714 saw the death of Queen Anne and the accession of George I. Upon George's enthronement, the Tory party in parliament rapidly fell out of favour with the new monarch. The Tories themselves were partly to blame, for they had overseen the signing with France of the Treaty of Utrecht which George, German by origin, felt was against Hanoverian interests (2). Sharpe states that George was intent upon removing the Tory ministers who had signed the treaty. His attitude was not helped by Tory propaganda which stressed the fact that a foreigner was now on the throne; this in addition to constant reminders from the Whigs of Tory links with the Jacobites. As Sharpe states, any ministry depended on royal support (3). Without that support a minister's career could be blocked or even terminated. Therefore, during 1714 the Tories were drummed from office and replaced with Whigs. These purges stretched from the upper reaches of parliament right down to local town and city government, with the Tories being removed from civil service posts and military positions. They lost power and influence.

The placing of people with a shared outlook in positions of power was a privilege which Walpole used to the full. With placemen able to sit in the Commons, Walpole was guaranteed support at a time when parliamentary whips were unheard of and party members were free to vote with or against their party. During Walpole's premiership the number of placemen reached 185, compared to 125 during Anne's reign (4). Even though Walpole's appointment of 185 was just a little more than that of the previous leader, Stanhope (between 155 and 170), it raised criticism, since it threatened to make parliament, in Speck's words, a 'rubber stamp' for the premier (5). Speck goes on to say that Walpole 'had at his disposal a more solid and reliable phalanx of court supporters in the Commons than any of his immediate predecessors' (6). But what of the House of Lords? Walpole exercised his powers to have sympathetic bishops and peers appointed to the upper house. Before long, Speck states, most of the bishops owed their offices to him. Even though the parliamentary opposition and political commentators levelled accusations of corruption against Walpole on account of his placemen, he was only taking advantage of a system which most premiers, both Whig and Tory, had exploited. It could perhaps be said that votes were bought with an array of appointments and pensions, but Walpole was just using the system to his advantage. A lengthy period of relative stability was the result.

Geoffrey Holmes believes that 'the pursuit of tranquillity and stability, social as well as political, had been an over-riding of [Walpole's] administration' (7). Sharpe observes that Walpole was content simply to 'exercise and enjoy power' (8). He believed that the key to success was to follow a peaceful foreign policy. Fighting wars was expensive. To finance such large undertakings entailed raising capital through either higher taxes or increased borrowing, or a mixture of the two. However, by the middle of his premiership, Walpole could point to a long period when England had not fought any wars and enjoyed a period of relative peace. This enabled the amount of government borrowing to fall. His financial abilities were one of Walpole's greatest aids.

Even before he came to power he showed his abilities with the instigation of the Sinking Fund and his handling of the South Sea Crisis. The basis on which the sinking fund was introduced was to reduce the interest payments on the national debt. Although the fund was Walpole's idea, it was actually introduced in 1717 by his rival, Stanhope. It was successful in keeping the national debt in check, and also provided funds to finance low land taxes on two occasions during Walpole's premiership. But it was perhaps his handling of the South Sea Crisis which launched Walpole's political career towards power.

Stanhope, not content with Walpole's scheme for reducing the country's debt, wanted a plan which would hasten the reduction. The scheme he favoured was the one put forward by the South Sea Company. After initially investing in the South Sea Company in June 1720, Walpole, on advice from his bankers, distanced himself from it. Speck states that recent findings indicate that while he initially opposed the scheme on behalf of his bank, Walpole actually approved of the plan in principle, only disagreeing with some of the details (9). When the company collapsed, Walpole, who had by then disowned the scheme, was asked to step in and salvage the country's finances. Seen as competent in financial affairs, he was expected to restore people's confidence in the government's credit. Walpole's handling of the resulting investigations saved the faces of many politicians. While it would have been in his interests to discredit as many of his opponents as possible, Walpole refrained from doing so. To expose all the transactions would reveal the involvement of many who gave him support. In addition to this, it would have exposed the dealings in the company by the King's friends and mistresses. He even gave support to his political rivals, Stanhope and Sunderland, both of whom were widely thought guilty of illegal involvement in the company. They were subsequently acquitted. After the inquiry Walpole was appointed Chancellor of the Exchequer, and, after Sunderland's dismissal, First Lord of the Treasury. The subsequent deaths of Stanhope and Sunderland removed the last obstacles to Walpole's ascendancy. Upon becoming premier, it was his financial skills which came to be viewed as one of his greatest assets.

One of the first major actions of Robert Walpole as prime minister was to introduce a simplified system of custom duties. Holmes describes Walpole's *forte* as lying not in 'striking originality but in making the original system work more efficiently and in rationalising it'; by expecting high standards from customs officials and increasing their jurisdiction to include Scotland, he made a real effort to reduce the high incidence of duty evasion (10). In addition to tightening up the customs service, Walpole removed excise duties from imported raw materials, and from many other imported goods. This gave a boost to the economy. Other measures which stimulated growth included simplified customs rates and the introduction of free ports and bonded warehouses. One of Walpole's principle aims was to keep land tax as low as possible. This he achieved in 1731 by bringing it down to one shilling in the pound. Perhaps the final chapter in his financial reforms came in 1733 with the introduction of excise duties on tobacco and wine. Although he introduced these taxes in the face of strong opposition (because of which later increases had to be abandoned), Walpole may well have been influenced by considerations other than the country's welfare. As Speck observes, Walpole kept land taxes low primarily to 'appease the country gentlemen,' and so keep their parliamentary support (11). Holmes detects a pattern in Walpole's financial policy, a 'long-term strategy for shifting the incidence of taxation away from land and property and on to consumable commodities' (12).

The longevity of Walpole's premiership depended, then, on several factors. The change of monarch in 1714 changed the balance of party power, while Walpole, a leading Whig, showed his financial talents with the introduction of the Sinking Fund and the easing of the South Sea Crisis. Having found favour with the King and seen the deaths of his two main rivals, his way was open. By maintaining a peaceful foreign policy and with no major legislation he was able to maintain a stability which British politics had not seen for many years; all this was aided by the Septennial Act, which meant that in his entire premiership he had to fight only three general elections. The overhaul of the country's finances, with no major conflicts to draw on them, meant that the economy flourished. Manufacturers and traders found it easier to operate with the improved import and export tariffs. Walpole showed his flair as a politician by using his powers of patronage to the full. Appointments in both houses of parliament were made to increase support and reduce opposition. It has often been said that Walpole was the first 'proper' prime minister, and there is some truth in the description, for he was a truly modern premier in his deployment of patronage, use of advisers, and attention to the popularity of low taxation among voters.

QUESTION: Account for the collapse of democracy in Germany between the two world wars.

During the period between 1918 and 1933, Germany was governed by the Weimar Republic whose constitution, written in 1919, was arguably the most democratic ever conceived. However this constitution had been laid on unstable foundations, which led to its downfall when attacked by Hitler's opposition in 1933.

There are many reasons why the Weimar Republic collapsed, one being the very constitution which established democracy in Germany. The constitution was simply too democratic for a country which had been used to a strong authoritarian government. The German people had been used to a hierarchical society and had grown to accept it. Whereas in the past they had been content to be led by the Kaiser and his ministers, now they were given universal suffrage and freedom of speech.

The system of proportional representation, although democratic, did not help to preserve democracy; instead, it led to weak, unstable governments, and made it possible for a number of small extremist parties to gain seats in the Reichstag. 'In 1932 27 parties contested the election and 15 gained seats in the Reichstag' (1). Because of this it became more difficult for any one party to gain a majority, so the republic came to consist of many different coalitions, which of their nature meant constant compromise and voter disaffection. The government was further weakened by the rapid turnover of Chancellors. Between 1918 and 1932 Germany had 14 Chancellors, so undermining public confidence in the government. In addition, 'between 1919 and 1933 there were 21 different cabinets' (2).

Another factor which weakened the power and prestige of parliament was the increased power accorded to the President. Article 48 gave the president the power of emergency decree which allowed him to overrule the Reichstag. For example, 'between 1930–1932 the Reichstag passed 29 relatively minor bills as opposed to 109 emergency decrees ratified by the President' (3). Also, the constitution could be changed by a two-thirds majority in the Reichstag, which would allow a leader with strong support the opportunity to change it. Hitler was able to do this in March 1933 when he gained a two-thirds majority through conservative support to give him the right to rule for four years without going to the Reichstag. This rendered parliament powerless and helped bring an end to the Republic.

After World War One, at the beginning of the Republic, Germany's economy was weak. Industry and agriculture had suffered during the war, and the loss of Alsace-Lorraine and the Tsar region weakened agriculture further. In addition, the reparation payments demanded by the Allies drained the economy. Germany could not afford these payments and many people did not see why they should be paid, especially the young, who hadn't fought in the war.

As the economy weakened, the government continued to issue banknotes, so fuelling inflation. By the end of 1924 Germany was suffering from hyper-inflation and banknotes were almost worthless. The value of money fell by the hour: 'in July 1918 the dollar had been worth 14 marks, and by November 1923 it was worth 4,200,000 marks' (4). There was great disaffection towards the government as many of the middle classes had been ruined, their savings rendered worthless. Workers starved as wages did not keep pace with inflation. The government was held responsible and people turned to the extreme left and right.

The problem was solved temporarily by a new currency being introduced – the Rentemark – and by the Dawes plan, whereby the Americans lent Germany short loans amounting to $800 million. However in the long term this meant that when there was another economic crisis the people would have no faith in the government.

Between 1924 and 1929 the economy recovered slowly, but Germany became reliant on short-term foreign loans. In 1928 Stresemann, the foreign minister, warned the government that 'Germany is dancing on a volcano. If in the short term credits are called in, a large section of our economy will collapse' (5). In 1929 the loans ended with the Wall Street Crash and depression took hold in Germany. Unemployment rose rapidly: 'By 1932 over six million people were out of work, which was almost one in three of the male working class' (6). The government unemployment insurance couldn't cope as it only had a fund sufficient to sustain 600,000 unemployed for three months. The people lost faith in the government and turned to the extreme parties for help. One way out of unemployment was to join one of the private armies of the extreme parties. Support for these parties grew rapidly: for example, in May 1928 the Nazis had just 12 seats and the Communists 54, but by July 1932 they had 230 and 89 respectively (7).

After the inflation crisis of 1923 the German people remembered how the government couldn't handle the crisis so they lost confidence in it.

During much of the Weimar Republic the main dissatisfaction with foreign policy stems from the Treaty of Versailles. The Republic was forced to sign at the end of the war or be forced back into it. Many Germans never forgave the Republic for signing it and it was an issue which haunted the government throughout its life. The treaty was very harsh on Germany, and as well as blaming Germany for the war it demanded high reparations in both goods and money. Also, much of the land which Germany had gained after unification was taken away. Germany was banned from making any alliance with Austria and was left feeling isolated. Hitler was later able to use the treaty against the government when he promised the people he would reverse it.

There were several incidents during the Republic which upset the people and paved the way for Hitler to mock the government and offer the people what they wanted to hear. The invasion of the Ruhr in January 1923 angered the Germans and resulted in the death of 132 people. The French invaded the Ruhr when Germany failed to deliver timber to France as part of the reparation payments.

The French interfered again in German affairs when in 1931 Bruining suggested an Austro-German customs union to try to solve the economic problems. France forced Germany to drop the scheme which made the government look as if it was being dictated to by France.

The Weimar republic collapsed for a number of reasons. It was used as a scapegoat for the problems which Germany faced at the end of World War One. Also a leader emerged from the sidelines who seemed to offer all the answers to Germany's problems. Hitler was able to use the system to gain what he wanted, to rule Germany.

It may have been possible to prevent the fall of the Weimar Republic. The Wall

Street Crash was a major blow to the economy and caused unrest among the people. Also the death of Stresemann was another blow to the economy. He had been getting the economy going and was slowly healing relations with the rest of Europe. However, Hitler was ready and waiting to lead the country and destroy democracy in Germany.

—3—

QUESTION: Was Stalinism the inevitable outcome of the Bolshevik Revolution?

There are two main theories relating to Stalinism and its source. The first sees it as a direct progression from Leninism and, therefore, a natural and inevitable progression of the Bolshevik Revolution. The second sees it as resulting from the politics and power ambitions of one man, Josef Stalin, and his ability to manipulate the system of the Bolshevik party. Evidence exists to confirm and contradict both theories. Christopher Hill warns of the danger of attempting to judge the 'successes or failures of the Soviet regime' (1). Any judgment must bear in mind that the Bolsheviks' attempt to build a socialist state was 'part of an experiment... made in conditions of quite exceptional difficulty' (2). Any experiment can produce an unexpected or unforeseen result, and it is the purpose of this essay to show how much could not have been foreseen in the aftermath of the revolution.

When the Bolsheviks came to power in October 1917 they were a small minority party whose power was confined to a small area of Russia. The country was bankrupted by war; the cities were starved of food and industry of raw materials. The Party which had been geared to revolution 'welded into a party united by a common theory' (3); it was ill-prepared to govern, and necessity as much as ideology prompted many of the early decisions. Lenin was prepared to change his ideas and policies to accommodate the needs of the moment; accordingly, many of the ideas associated with Stalinism can be found in the early years of Bolshevik government, and in particular the period known as 'War Communism'. As R. Medvedev points out, however, 'there is still the question of different historical circumstances... we have reason to suppose that Lenin would never have gone as far as Stalin' (4) To cite this period as an example of Leninism and then to describe Stalinism as a continuation of the same policies is to ignore the background that brought it about.

Most historians agree that the Bolshevik party had two distinctive characteristics, its centralism and its discipline: both were crucial weapons in the fight for survival against forces both within Russia and outside it. However, when combined with the bureaucratic power of the party they could also provide the means for a ruthless individual, suitably manipulative, to control both the party and the country.

Martin McCauley notes that Lenin 'was fascinated by administrative detail and devoted more time to government than to party matters' (5). He goes on to explain how Lenin, as Prime Minister, took over many of the structures and practices of the old government; he notes that Lenin's prime concern, as a Marxist, was the control of institutions rather than their structure. As a result the line between government and party was always blurred, but it was power of the party to make appointments across the broad spectrum of government, party and soviets which strengthened the party bureaucracy. By 1924 Lenin became aware of the dangers both to the party and the state that Stalin's control of the bureaucratic machine posed, but he was taken ill before he could take steps to remedy it.

If the strength of the party lay in its centralism and discipline, then perhaps its greatest weakness was the failure of its internal structures to appoint new leaders or regulate their time in power. The party had evolved as a revolutionary group, a small political elite of which Lenin was the undisputed and unelected leader. The necessity of maintaining secrecy in an illegal organization had obviously precluded any form of election of officers by the membership as a whole, and the result was self-election by the elite. Roy Medvedev suggests that while no one could replace Lenin in 1917, by the '20s and '30s there were several leaders who could have headed the party (6). However, for a variety of reasons Lenin appears never to have made plans for choosing a new leader, or restricting the period for which any individual could hold office. His illness caught the party off guard and his early death in 1924 left the party with no obvious single successor.

From the bitter and jealous wrangling amongst the leading revolutionaries which followed Lenin's death, Stalin eventually emerged as the leader in 1929. Alan Wood sums up Stalin's accumulation of bureaucratic power, his establishment of himself as 'a crucial cog in government' through his willingness to take on the more mundane and unglamorous duties (7). These duties included Commissariat for Nationalities, Head of the Workers' and Peasants' Inspectorate, and, finally, the newly-created post of General Secretary of the Communist Party.

The needs of government and the ability of the party to retain power necessitated the expansion of the party membership in 1919. As a result of this rapid expansion the political elitism of the party, as advocated by Lenin, was lost. Many of the new members had little or no knowledge of Marxist theory, and in the future many of these new members would owe their allegiance not to the party but to the man who had granted them party membership: that man was Stalin.

The sheer size of Russia must not be overlooked when assessing the revolution or its aftermath. In 1917 the Bolsheviks were a minority organisation controlling only a minute area of the country: the Civil War was fought as much to hold on to their power and expand it, as it was to repel outside forces. The Bolsheviks proved themselves every bit as ruthless in their methods of holding on to power as the Tsars before them. Many of the methods used by them during the periods known as the Red Terror and the Civil War – censorship, secret police, brutal repression, confiscation of property in the name of the state – had been used by the Tsarist government. These same measures would also form the background against which the policies of Stalin's 'Socialism in One Country' would be enforced.

That the people of Russia were prepared to exchange the autocratic dictatorship of the Tsar for the dictatorship of a single party must in part be due to their lack of any tradition of democratic process or debate. The abdication of Nicholas II had created a power vacuum which the unelected provisional government had failed to fill adequately. The Bolshevik seizure of power in Petrograd had been unopposed by a people weary of war and the problems it had caused: they welcomed any person or party offering to end their troubles. Lenin's simple call for 'peace, bread and land' appeared to do just that.

Over 80 percent of the population in 1917 were illiterate peasants, brought up to perceive the Tsar as the 'father of the nation'. This predisposition towards an individual ruler may explain the ease with which first the 'cult of Lenin' and later the 'cult of Stalin' were introduced. Lenin himself, as Medvedev points out, was 'always ready to subordinate his personal interests and ambitions of the party.... Stalin... was fanatically dedicated to the quest for personal power' (8).

From the outset Lenin was prepared to change or modify his ideas in order to build the socialist state, hence the change from War Communism to NEP at the tenth party congress in March 1921. This was seen by many in the party as a backward step but Lenin stressed its necessity. To allay further opposition or dissent within the party Lenin banned factionalism: henceforth any issue must be discussed by the entire party and not by individuals, groups or platforms. Expulsion was the punishment for infringing this rule. This ban effectively killed off any form of democracy within the party. Lenin saw it as only a temporary measure until the political situation stabilised and the party accepted NEP. In reality it closed the door on democracy, and created a loophole through which a party dictator could emerge.

The social and political background of the Russian people arguably made them more likely to accept a one-party state as offered by the Bolsheviks. In assessing the problems of government confronting the Bolsheviks, a strong, well-disciplined, centralised bureaucracy seemed to be the answer to successful control of the country. While all the apparatus of the police state appears to have been in place by 1920, there is no evidence that it was intended as part of a long-term policy. It can also be argued that the same apparatus had long existed and been used by the Tsars. The emergence of one unelected man as supreme leader, and the unlimited power at his disposal, seem to have occurred through oversight rather than design.

The Bolshevik experiment was carried out in difficult conditions. Many short-term decisions, apparently practical, were to prove disastrous in the long term. The failure of the Bolshevik party itself to remain democratic, together with its reliance on centralized bureaucracy, compounded these problems and permitted the emergence of a dictator.

Stalinism resulted from a combination of factors, chief of which was the party's oversight in failing to provide an adequate leadership structure. Any political party which fails to devise a method of choosing its leader and to place limits of power and tenure on that leader leaves itself open to dictatorship. The combination of policies, dictated by events as much as ideology, the over-centralising of power, and the socio-historic background of Russia itself, all contributed. Stalinism was not an inevitable result of the Bolshevik revolution, but rather a result of the Bolshevik party's oversights in strategic areas which allowed one man's political ambition and cunning to gain him absolute power.

Exercises

In this section we will look at different aspects of the essays you have just been reading:

- Introductions
- Paragraphing
- Use of sources
- Conclusions
- Answering the question

Introductions

1. Compare the introductions of essays 2 and 3. Which of the following is true of which introduction?

   (i) distinguishes between different approaches to the question
   (ii) excludes simple narrative information
   (iii) shows how the essay is going to relate to the question
   (iv) avoids simply re-stating the question
   (v) assigns a single function to each sentence
   (vi) leads the reader into the main body of the essay
   (vii) declares what argument is going to be advanced

2. Obviously one of these essays has the better introduction! Now look at the beginning of essay 1. How does that compare? (use the list of features given above).

3. If we go back to the introduction to essay 3, we can see that it has a distinct structure, based, like all good writing, on clear sentence functions. There are seven sentences, and their functions might be described like this:

   (i) enumerate possible answers to the question
   (ii) summarise first possible answer
   (iii) summarise second possible answer
   (iv) give equal status to each possible answer
   (v) state terms of a simplistic approach to the subject (it is usual to quote a critical source here)
   (vi) explain why such an approach is simplistic
   (vii) state the key theme to be expanded on in the rest of the essay

Use this as a working model. Obviously there will be occasions when the order or nature of the functions differs, but this is a good procedure to follow at first.

4 Look again at the introduction to essay 1. Try to improve it by using the model set out above.

5 Historians prefer a plain style: crisp sentences with easily identifiable functions, accurate and impersonal vocabulary, precise reference to time and circumstance. Here is an introduction by a student who has yet to grasp these essentials. Try to put the passage in order by cutting down the sentences, putting them in the right order, and changing the words where necessary:

QUESTION: Assess the economic and social impact of enclosures in the late eighteenth and early nineteenth centuries.

Gordon Smith says in his magisterial study of Norfolk farming, published in 1957, that enclosure was the single most beneficial thing for Norfolk people around the 1800s because it increased the production of many foods such as cereal and wheat and made a lot of farmers very prosperous, but I think it was an absolute disaster because it changed the social system and meant that people who lived in cottages, who were called cottagers, lost rights over common land and with it their means of subsistence, like the squatters who were suddenly evicted from land which they had occupied for a very long time indeed. It's just like new-age travellers today in comparison. It was all fairly inevitable, really, with the growth of towns and cities and the French wars, which made everything more expensive, but there are lots of different ways of trying to understand its impact.

Paragraphing

A good introduction, we have seen, makes it clear immediately that different approaches to the question have been grasped. Good paragraphing will show that those aspects are being explored in an orderly and discriminating way.

1. Like introductions, paragraphs have a clear structure, although that structure is likely to be more variable. Look at the second paragraph of essay 3. The sentences perform the following functions:

   (i) topic sentence (nature of Bolshevik power base)
   (ii) background detail for topic sentence
   (iii) consequence of topic sentence
   (iv) detail of consequence
   (v) counter-argument, quoting an authority
   (vi) conclusion, balancing counter-argument against topic and consequence

Now you try. Write a paragraph about a topic in history that you're familiar with, following the list of functions given above.

2 Not all paragraphs will look like the one you have just imitated. Turn to paragraphs four ('Martin McCauley notes') and five ('If the strength of the party') of essay 3 and see if you can break down their different sentence functions.

3 An essay is not just a collection of paragraphs: they all have to fit together. It follows that the topic sentence will often stress the relationship of the new paragraph with what has come before – preferably the previous paragraph! Find some topic sentences in any of the three essays which seem, in this light, especially successful or otherwise.

4 Paragraphs have functions, like the sentences they contain. They might:

   (i) underline an existing point by giving further evidence
   (ii) qualify a point made earlier by citing further evidence
   (iii) explore the consequences of a point already made
   (iv) establish a parallel with a point already made
   (v) extend the application of a point already made

Can you find examples of these paragraph functions in any of the essays?

In most cases, functions (ii), (iii) and (v) are the ones most likely to lead to a controlled, argumentative essay. Accumulating evidence (i) and establishing parallels (iv) can be a substitute for real thought. When you plan your essay you need to think about the different points you want to make in terms of paragraph functions. Only then can you be confident that you are tackling the question in an orderly way. Be sure to do the exercise in question 4 on Answering the Question, below (p.92).

Use of sources

Quoting sources is an essential part of demonstrating that you are on top of a subject. The point is not to blunt your personal awareness of historical issues, but to sharpen them up, to show that you can account for different points of view in developing your argument. Remember that you have to record critical citations properly, as set out in Core Element 6 (pp.38–45).

1 What do you notice about the way critical sources are used in the three essays?

2 Like paragraphing, source quotation should be dynamic, an occasion for saying something more. It follows that you should add something to the words you quote, rather than just relying on them for moral support or cosmetic effect. You could, for example,

   (i) highlight a particular word or phrase that is useful
   (ii) build in to your own sentence a useful word or phrase
   (iii) sum up the usefulness of a quoted opinion
   (iv) explore the consequences of a quoted opinion
   (v) identify or question the assumptions behind a quoted opinion
   (vi) disagree, wholly or partially, with a quoted opinion
   (vii) play two contrasting opinions off against each other

Can you find examples of these in the three essays? Is there a difference between the practice of essay 3 and that of the others? Try to identify moments where the students could have used one of the functions above, but didn't.

3 It is very important to use the right language to signal your relationship to quoted material: as in life in general, you don't want to be too brusque or too reticent. Look at essay 3 and make a note of the words and phrases used to signal the functions you have identified from the list above.

⚠️ *A golden rule with quotations: if you are going to quote a long passage, you must say a good deal about the quotation to justify its inclusion.*

Conclusions

We've already looked briefly at conclusions in Writing Brief Essays, Core Element 4. Have another look at what you found there and see if you can apply it to the endings of the essays printed here.

1 Which seems to you the most successful of the three conclusions, and why?

2 How could any of the three conclusions have been improved?

3 None of the three endings uses the kind of vocabulary you might expect: 'In conclusion', 'finally', etc. How *do* they signify an ending?

4 Good conclusions (to repeat a familiar point), like introductions and paragraphs, have a structure. Look at the final paragraph of essay 3. The sentences perform the following functions:

  (i) topic (principal answer to the question)
  (ii) consequences of topic
  (iii) factors affecting or explaining the topic
  (iv) conclude by matching phrasing of the question to the topic

In practice, (iii) might well, and perhaps should, come before (ii), but the stated order works well enough here.

⚠️ *Historians value the summarising function of conclusions. Don't introduce new material into your final paragraph!*

5 Try to tidy up the conclusion to essay 2 by using the list of functions given above.

Answering the question

You've already come to some judgment about how well each of the essays answers the question set. You may have noticed that there are different kinds of question.

1 Look at the following essay questions. Are there different types?

(a) Account for the collapse of democracy in Germany, 1918–1933.
(b) Was Stalinism the inevitable outcome of the Bolshevik Revolution?
(c) Account for the longevity of Sir Robert Walpole's political ascendancy.
(d) Assess the economic and social impact of enclosures in the late eighteenth and early nineteenth centuries.
(e) Was the Revolution of 1688 an inevitable consequence of the ambiguities of the Restoration Settlement?
(f) "The term 'Revolution' has seldom been more badly misapplied" (Davies). Do you agree with this assessment of the British Republic?

---

2 You've no doubt found that history is much concerned with causes and effects. However, even in 'effect' type essays there is a great deal of 'cause' type material. Can you find some examples of this in essays 1 and 3?

3 How do you explain this phenomenon? Why so much 'cause' when the question is about 'effect'?

4 'Cause and effect' obviously doesn't mean that a good history essay will simply narrate what happened before an event and what happened after it: narration is the best path to a low mark! A good essay will sort out its priorities: the most important considerations will receive the bulk of attention. Try to reconstruct the plan of essay 1 in order to understand how the writer has arranged his priorities.

5 Two of the questions in the list above are probably more demanding than the others: 'Was *x* the inevitable outcome of *y*?' demands a slightly sharper focus. Why?

6 Go back to essay 3, which answers this more difficult kind of question very successfully. How does it deal with the problems posed by the word 'inevitable'?

7 It follows that when you begin to answer a question you must do three things:

(i) Consider the question as a whole: remember that a claim is being made that you must debate. Try rephrasing the claim a few times so that you're completely happy about what it means. Remember that debating a claim means neither swallowing it whole nor discarding it: seek to explain why it is useful as well as limited.

(ii) Consider carefully the key words in the question – these will direct you towards the areas you need to cover, and help you to give an exact answer. Essay 3 succeeds because it considers seriously the word 'inevitable'.

(iii) Remember that in any 'effect' type question, you have to think about how the *effects* of an event are partly determined by its *causes*.

Summary: a procedure to follow

So far we've been looking at different aspects of history essays. Now we need to pull everything together in the form of a procedure that you can follow when you write a history essay. Try following these ten steps:

1 Break down the question (see number 7 in Answering The Question, p.92, above), making sure that you understand it. When there is a selection of questions, don't choose one immediately without thinking about the others; it might turn out to be more difficult.

2 Research: condense all the different areas that the question is asking you to consider.

3 Sort out any areas of controversy where you can draw on the work of published historians. Remember that you are debating a claim.

4 Decide which of the different areas have priority in your account.

5 Plan: refer back to the Paragraphing section you've just done (p.88) and sort out the relationships between the different points you want to make. Make sure that you

have enough material for each point to construct a well-made paragraph. Remember to show an awareness of the different views that could be taken of the topic. It might be helpful to explain your plan to a friend at this stage – this can be a good way of finding out if it is really logical.

6 Write an introduction that will set out your agenda clearly – check against the Introductions section (pp.87–8) you have just worked through.

7 Get writing! Remember to structure each paragraph coherently – check against the Paragraphing section.

8 When you get there, remember to make your conclusion correspond to the pattern suggested in the Conclusions section. Don't add anything new at the last minute.

9 Make sure you have referenced the essay fully, in accordance with the guidelines set out in the Core Element 6.

10 Proofread! Nothing irritates a marker more than careless errors. Try reading the essay out loud to see if it sounds right. Your logical and indulgent friend will appreciate the experience enormously!

Essays in Sociology

Sample Essays

What follows is a sample of essays submitted by first-year students of Sociology over the past year. There are three essays, and each one gained a different pass mark, A, B, or C. Satisfy yourself that you're familiar with the contents of the Marking Criteria section of this book (pp.49 51) and then read through all of the essays, trying to decide which essay gained which mark. You might like to make a note of any sections or passages that fulfill particular aspects of the criteria, or that appear especially successful or otherwise for any other reasons. Think, for example, about how well the essay answers the question set. After the essays, there are some exercises for you to complete.

⚠️ *No bibliographies are included in these examples. Never omit bibliographies in your own work! You will see from these essays that Sociologists favour the Author + Date form of referencing.*

—1—

QUESTION: Explore the role played by social institutions in the formation of gender.

Although the family plays a large part in forming gender identity, it is not the only source of learning. Books, comics, magazines and television all portray certain identities which are more suitable for one gender than the other.

For the purposes of this essay, the media will be focused on to see if it plays a part in the creation of our social identities in relation to gender.

The media is a major socialising agent influencing people's attitudes and behaviour, and it is also an agent of gender role socialisation.

According to numerous sociologists, the media reflects and maintains two dominant images of women. The first is the housewife/mother image, and the second the woman as sex object. This is where the media creates an 'ideal of femininity'. The housewife/mother image is a major image portrayed in magazines and advertisements. This is mainly found in women's magazines which are overwhelmingly concerned with diet and fashion stories, in which the ideal woman is always slim and beautiful. The other stories in such magazines are all concerned with traditional gender roles, for example the home or child development.

Ferguson (1983) suggests that recent investigations of women's magazines show that today many magazines have changed their style to suit changing realities and beliefs, without trying to challenge the overall subordination of women.

Research by Durkin and Akhtar (1990s) confirms earlier findings that roles allocated to the sexes on television are often highly distorted. Males tend to be assertive, tough and dynamic, while females tend to be soft, deferent and physically attractive. Recent statistics show that males on television out-number females by two to one. Although more men are shown on television, Tuchman (1981) states that the typical male image is always of a single male.

In advertising the case is much the same in supporting traditional gender roles. Women are seen using the new vacuum cleaner or showing the new nappy, but the voice explaining the product is nearly always male, assuring the would-be customer of the scientifically-tested quality of the product.

In soap operas the pattern is much the same. The main stars of about 14% of the early evening programmes are women: most of these are aged under thirty and have typical female jobs or are housewives. If a woman is shown to have a successful career, then sooner or later she will either be made redundant or leave her job to start a family.

Durkin and Akhtar carried their research further to look at the effects of television sex stereotypes on children. It was found that the children use what they see on television to reinforce their own picture of the two sexes.

The media also creates an ideal of femininity. This means that the media assumes that we all want to and can conform to its definitions of femininity and masculinity. Those who don't conform are lacking or portrayed in offensive stereotypes. One of the most common concerns about the media today is the way it stereotypes people. Perkins (1979) argues that stereotypes, although simple in form, are in fact compressed, shorthand ways of referring to quite complex social relationships. Males and females in television programmes typically do find themselves playing roles which supposedly come naturally to them. The stereotyping which takes place in these situations aims to suggest that such differences are in-born. It also goes on to re-inforce the view that a woman's social position is caused by differences in aptitude or ability. In doing this it enforces the possibility that such differences may be the effect of their inferior position in a male-dominated society.

Golding (1974), however, produces evidence that facts of social structure and social institutions intervene with great effect in the process of counteracting traditional gender roles. It is even possible that the movement towards greater gender equality owes a great deal to the publicity given by way of the mass media. Rogers and Shoemaker (1971) argue that the effects of the mass media on gender role enforcement should be considered at a level beyond that of the individual audience and of individual behaviour. Other social institutions are under pressure to adapt or respond in some way, to make full use of the opinions offered by the mass media. In the process their views are likely to alter over time.

Thomson (1964) carried out his research some years ago, but offers the same view of gender as present-day writers. The media makes stimulating television, women's magazines, newspapers, film and pop music, but it is used as much as a tool of repression as of enlightenment.

However, many sociologists say that it is wrong to believe any medium has a direct influence on its audience. Furthermore, it is more likely that the medium will have the power to change opinion about unimportant matters, as opposed to serious and important ones (hence the success of advertising for soap powders against its failure for a political party). It is more likely that people will accept from the media what they are already predisposed to agree with and reject what they are not in sympathy with. Klapper (1960), however, believes that in certain circumstances, with certain carefully structured messages directed at susceptible people, the media can have a direct effect. A quote by Professor Klapper can be related to the reason why the media plays a part in forming gender identities:

'Mass communication is either impotent or harmless. Its reinforcement effect is potent and socially important, and it reinforces, with fine distinction, both socially desirable and socially undesirable predispositions. Which are desirable and which are not is, of course, a matter of opinion.'

Cohen and Young (1973) observe that 'The mass media provide a major source of knowledge in a segregated society of what consensus actually is and what is the nature of deviation from it. They conjure up for each group, with its limited stock of social knowledge, what "everyone else" believes.'

This view has been subject to much criticism in that the media structures the world for us, helping us to make sense of it. A supporter of this view is Taviss (1969), who argues that media content reflects dominant social values, interests and concerns to the extent that the media can be used to measure social change. Numerous studies have been concerned with the media as agents of socialisation. One of the primary concerns has been with the impact of its presentation of female stereotypes. Friedan (1963) was perhaps the first to draw attention to the potentially harmful effects of stereotyped gender presentation. In studies of sex role socialisation, the assumption

97

is made that the media do act as agents of socialization. Many editors feel that readers, especially readers of fiction, claim that traditional stereotypes and expectations are what readers want. An emphasis on young, single dominant-group heroines is part of the conventional structure of the romance, just as an emphasis on single, virile, and fearless males characterises detective stories.

A shortcoming in much of the early research in to the mass media has been researched by McQuail (1977), who suggests that the media is seen by many to have almost magical powers to alter the ideas and behaviour of its audience. This notion he called the 'hypodermic model': media messages are seen as directly injected into the minds of individuals who are powerless to resist. There are two main assumptions, common to much of the early research. The first is often referred to as the idea of 'mass society'. This implies that individuals who make up society are entirely on their own with the media as their only point of reference. The second assumption is more psychological than sociological in its way of thinking. Wertham (1953) states that people take roles they find in the media. This was the beginning of the debate as to whether individuals are affected by the presentation of violence in the media.

Although many media sociologists have now abandoned the 'hypodermic' model, in recent years it has been taken up again by the feminist movement, who have highlighted the effects on male behaviour of media depictions of sexuality and violence and their consequences for women. Hall (1978) shows that the media represents the major means by which individuals, groups and classes construct an understanding of the lives, meanings, practices and values of other individuals, classes, genders and groups, and acquire a picture of how the whole of 'social reality' hangs together to form our identities. Our own identities as men and women are constructed by imposing a selective framework which may exclude alternative interpretations or meanings. One drawback with this is the assumption that all members of a society are in agreement over a range of norms, values and ideas. It is when this agreement is broken that confusion arises in the formation of our social identities.

In conclusion, the media is a principle agent of socialisation and in the formation of our social identities. The media helps to socialise males and females to adopt their socially acceptable gender roles and the feminists argue that the media creates social identities in a climate where violence against women is tolerated and male sexual dominance is considered to be the norm.

—2—

QUESTION: Explore the role played by social institutions in the formation of gender.

Any exploration of the role played by social institutions in the creation of social identity requires an initial definition of the concepts involved. Such definitions change. In Sociology, there has been a shift away from the functionalist views of thinkers such as Mead and Talcott Parsons, who saw the social institution as a channel through which the main concerns and activities of a society were organised and fundamental needs met. Now the consensus is to view the social institution as the embodiment of a relatively stable value system which incorporates changing patterns of behaviour. This identification of the social institution with the value systems of society coincides with Berger's argument that social identity is 'socially bestowed, socially sustained and socially transformed' (Berger 1984). Whilst there is no clear consensus as to what constitutes social identity, one of the most plausible ones is that which gives priority to the expectations attached to social roles inhabited by an individual, so internalised through socialisation. This assignment will attempt to examine the role played by social institutions such as education and the family in the creation of gender identity. While concentrating primarily on gender as a feminist issue, it will further recognise that a specific gender role is also imposed on men by a patriarchal society.

Gender, as opposed to sex, is a social construct. While sex may be considered to have a biological basis and therefore to cross cultural boundaries, gender is subject to historical and cross-cultural variation. Feminist writers such as Oakley have identified the change in women's roles from pre-industrial to modern capitalist society and have argued that there has been a limitation on women's roles with the development of a 'cash economy', where more value is placed on paid work – usually undertaken by men – than on the unpaid domestic duties undertaken by women. In addition, with the change from the family as a unit of production to a unit of consumption, women's roles have become more confined, so that in the nineteenth century there was a gradual change, filtering down through the class system, which envisaged as ideal the man working in order to support his wife and family. Feminists have argued that it is the housewife role which has become the accepted norm for women, and even when paid work outside the home is undertaken, this is seen as an adjunct to a woman's primary role as wife and mother. Apart from this economic explanation for women's subservient position, feminists such as Taylor have cited the importance of their reproductive role: 'Instead of defining just one difference between men and women, women's ability to bear children is used to define their entire lives. It is used to create and justify a role for women that extends their responsibility for caring for children far beyond the nine months of pregnancy.' (Taylor, 1985)

However, there is much anthropological evidence to challenge the idea of 'natural' female roles in patriarchal societies. Margaret Mead's 1935 study, 'Sex and Temperament in Three Primitive Societies', provides an example of three societies where gender roles differed greatly from those of Western society. In one tribe, the

Arapesh, both males and females were reared to develop what in Western society would be considered typically feminine qualities; while in a second tribe, the Mundugumor, both males and females exhibited the stereotypically male qualities of aggressiveness and arrogance. A third tribe, the Tchambuli, reversed typical Western gender roles, with the females in charge of the economic life of the tribe while the males were considered the 'weaker' sex. Malinowski (1929) also reported a reversal of western male and female roles in his study of Trobriand islanders where women subjected men to 'gang rape'. Oakley (1972), in a review of such anthropological studies, concluded that while most societies differentiated between male and female roles, there were vast differences in what was considered 'normal' for each gender. More recently, Lee and Daly (1987) have argued that the oppressive nature of male/female relations has paralleled the development of societies from 'hunter/gatherer' stage, to simple agrarian, to more industrialised societies. They cite the egalitarian nature of gender relations in the Kung San tribe of Botswana where a hunter/gatherer mode of existence is still in operation. However, they fail to address the possibility of the internalisation and acceptance of social identities in their account of the female tribe members, who are said to be 'excellent mothers' and to 'keenly desire children.'

There is a stark contrast between the functionalist view of the family as a socialising agency and that of Marxists. Functionalists see the family as an institution which provides stability and benefits for both society and for its individual members. Marxists, however, emphasise the role of the family, and the primary role played by women within it, in the maintenance and reproduction of the capitalist system. However, it is feminist writers who stress the dysfunctional effects of the family as experienced by women.

Women have a dual role within the family: that of producing a new generation of workers and providing for the needs of the current generation. Feminist writers such as Abbott and Wallace (1990) have argued that during this process women lose their individual sense of identity and 'often become seen as an appendage of their husbands and children... having no separate social identity of their own'. This is in contrast to men, who are seen to take their main identity from employment. Oakley's 1981 account of the poet Sylvia Plath demonstrates how thoroughly the supportive role is internalised by women, as Plath rejoices in the success of her husband: 'I am so happy his book is accepted first. It will make it much easier for me when mine is accepted.'

The family, therefore, may be seen as a prime socialising agent in the formation and maintenance of social identity. Studies such as those of Lake (1975) have demonstrated how, commencing from earliest babyhood, babies are treated differently by their carers according to their (perceived) gender, reinforcing stereotypical expectations of gender-appropriate behaviour. This is continued throughout childhood, while the effects of modelling and observation of gender-appropriate behaviour has been documented by such psychologists as Bandura and Mischel (1967 & 1970). As Oakley (1981) concludes, 'the institutions of marriage and the family are today seen as the prisons in which women's psychological inferiority is imbibed and ensured.' Moving away from the feminist viewpoint a little, a parallel may be drawn here with the socialisation of boys within the family who internalise their own masculine identity of superiority from the same source where girls learn their dependence.

100

The socialising process begun within the family is continued in the education system. Arnott (1986) has commented on the inevitability of differences within the education system: 'if adult life is sex-segregated, it would seem only natural that to devise an education system that catered for a sex-segregated world.'

Although appearing to start with an initial advantage (girls perform slightly better than boys at reading at the age of eight) this is soon eroded, with boys and girls performing more or less equally on maths tests by the age of eleven. Secondary and higher education see a widening gap between male and female achievement. At secondary level and beyond there is also a marked preponderance of girls in arts subjects and of boys in science. The current trend is towards some erosion of these differences, but, as Harding (1982) reports, there is almost a complete male absence from traditional female subjects such as cookery and needlework, and a similar female absence from subjects such as woodwork, metalwork and technology. Blunden (1983) argues that 'the subjects in which girls predominate are those originally introduced into the curriculum to prepare them either for domestic service or home management'. This situation also contributes towards the sexual division of labour as they are often seen as less marketable skills. Women are therefore not only disadvantaged by their role within the family as primarily home-makers and carers, but are also being educated for this role. Skeggs (1986) concludes that they bear some responsibility for this: 'By continuing to take these subjects girls contribute towards making themselves less available for employment in high status occupations and thus reproduce the historical legacy of state education as a pre-requisite for family life.' The power of institutionalised practice is nonetheless evident, both internally and externally.

Other institutions such as the media are instrumental in creating and reinforcing gender identity. We are bombarded with images which show women in the housewife role and men in the world of work or driving fast cars. There are, of course, exceptions to these stereotypical images: women are shown as managers, men appear holding babies. However, we are all aware that these are deviations from the norm, and even the welfare policies of the state are formulated on the basis that women are dependent on men.

The role played by social institutions in the formation of gender identity is a crucial one. Recent sociological thinking has been largely dominated by the feminist perspective, which has concentrated on the socialisation of women into the housewife role. However, it is important to recognise that the foil to this feminine identity is the socialisation of males into the stereotypical role of breadwinner. The primary socialising agency in this capacity is the family, which legitimises the confinement of women to the home. As feminist writers such as Sharpe (1976) have argued, there is a vast difference in the relationship of men and women to home. For a woman, home is where her identity becomes 'lost, submerged within her caring', while for a man the home provides a refuge from the world of work, which, despite its stresses, provides him with an independent identity. The socialisation begun in childhood, as male and female roles are modelled and internalised, is continued by the secondary socialising agency of the education system. Stanworth (1983), in an analysis of gender differences encoded within education, concluded, 'Girls may follow the same curriculum as boys – may sit side by side with boys in classes taught by the same teachers – and yet emerge from school with the implicit understanding that the world is a man's world in which women can and should take second place.' Other social institutions such as the media and the welfare system legitimate and reinforce the social identities formed through the socialising agencies of education and the family.

The formation of social identity is a complex process requiring the agency of social institutions for its conception and maintenance. Such identity is based on gender stereotyping with passive, gentle qualities being attributed to females and more active, aggressive qualities being attributed to males. Despite the progress made by the feminist movement, and recognition of the patriarchal nature of modern British society, these stereotypes are still current and have been internalised as the ideal social identities to be achieved by many, both male and female.

—3—

QUESTION: Drawing upon appropriate sociological examples, discuss the importance of social relations in constraining and empowering social identities.

The main thrust of this essay will concern itself with women and especially women in the workplace. It is with this mind that I refer to Joshi's article, 'The Changing Form of Women's Economic Dependency' (1989), in which she argues that although women have made the step away from being financially dependent on men, independence has not yet been achieved, mainly due to inequalities of earning power.

Throughout my research into this topic one concept has appeared consistently: power, at once physical, psychological, and economic. It is the social power of one group over another which usually constrains the identity-forming process. It would seem that most gender-related issues are concerned with the exploitation of women, whether in the workplace or at home. As recently as 1850, women, irrespective of class, had no legal status whatever and it did not become legal for women to retain any money or property upon marriage until 1870. It was only at the beginning of this century, when the working class began to diversify into other jobs, which then caused a shortage of servants, that lower middle class wives were forced to take on light household duties and child care. Oakley (1974) saw this as a turning point for all women: 'Where the middle class wife had been idle, she now worked, and in this transition lies one explanation of housework's modern status as non-work.'

The importance of World War Two in defining women's dual role as private and public worker must not be under-estimated, for then a woman's place was also in the munitions factories. With the decline in heavy excavating industries, the new light engineering developments brought jobs to the people for the first time, rather than expecting workers to travel to raw material sites for mining or shipbuilding. The new jobs were local and involved the need for deftness on a fairly dull, repetitive basis. Thereby the ideal part-time, low-paid jobs for women were established. As an individual, a woman may despair of the personal constraints on her gender/power position and yet as a group women have come an extremely long way in just over a century.

If we return to Joshi's article, she states that in the 30 year period after the war the proportion of women in the workforce increased by 12% to 45%. Although this is quite a phenomenal rise over a short period, the really startling fact is that all of this increase was in part-time employment. Since the Victorian era when childbirth was abandoned as a full-time career, Joshi implies that the dual role of child carer and paid worker has been accepted by more and more women of the group who care for younger pre-school children. Yet women have also been ever-mindful that the family is the mainstay of substantial relationships and must always be a priority.

In the 1981 Census it was shown that 75% of women workers could be classified into just four of the sixteen available work categories, all four of which were either caring or menial roles. The caring concept is actively reinforced and even exploited by the fact that the country community care of the disabled relies exclusively on the unpaid efforts of the women involved in the various relationships of wife, daughter, and so on, so inhibiting any thoughts of self-interest and personal desire within this group.

Even with the Equal Pay Act of 1970, which raised 'equal pay' to the level of 75% of the male rate, the ethos of pin-money remained. There are so many insidious roots to this notion: the anticipation of domesticity and child-rearing encouraged in girls (MacRobbie 1980); the logical notion that as the husband has more earning potential it makes more sense for the wife to stay at home, so reducing her earning potential further in future years. Joshi suggests that the reason for continued low pay is twofold: first, gendered division of labour; second, unequal treatment of male and female labour within the labour market. The latter is self-evident from the information given above, while the former is also well documented: Gershuny *et al.* (1986) stated that women work an extra 16 hours unpaid per week compared with men. In fact the socialisation of women has been so successful that among those women who work full-time 90% still do most or all of the family cooking and shopping.

Socialisation has an extremely important part to play in the formation of gender roles. In a recent television programme entitled 'Gender Subordination', the problem was looked at globally and it was shown that in the very poorest parts of Africa 'dirt farmers', who have no social position, work a six-hour morning toiling in the fields, while their wives work a fifteen-hour day in the fields and are still responsible for household and child-care duties. This perhaps suggests that even when humanity cannot sink any lower, women will still be found at the bottom. Gita Sen, a sociologist from India, suggests that in her country the subordinate position of women begins at birth with the feeding practices arranged for boys and girls. Irrespective of class, girls are considered secondary to boys and are treated as such; the problem is compounded by the fact that as the elderly are also revered in India, the wife is constrained not only by the wishes of her husband but by those of her mother-in-law, which tends to perpetuate the problem of discrimination throughout the generations. This type of discrimination is not confined to Third World countries. Fagot (1978) shows that female traits are still seen in Western societies as a weakness and that parents are more willing to accept a dominant, aggressive daughter than a passive, dependent son.

Sen highlighted the matches industry. India is the largest producer of matches, and the vast majority of workers were women who worked in appalling conditions, squatting on the floor for many hours a day. As soon as the industry was mechanised, the women were dismissed and men worked the machinery. The women lost out because of the power structure which is evident in many developing countries. Policy making, implementation, and distribution of resources are controlled by men and therefore women's input and interests are marginalised.

All is not doom and gloom, however, for there is an active faction who are taking the unusual step for Indian women of demanding family planning for all in the hope that if women are not continually rearing children they may be empowered to realise their own potential. This all sounds similar to our own history. Sen was asked to comment on which development issues enhanced the question of women's rights: she pointed out the futility of integrating women into a male-dominated social structure which did not benefit women in any way.

If we return to our own country and look at the article by Barrie Clement, 'Women in professions "fighting a sex war" ' (Appendix 1), it would seem from the title as if women are rising up in a riotous mass. However, when looked at a little closer it appears that the author was only commenting on a single survey of 600 people from one recruitment agency. Clement stressed at the beginning of the article that although more female graduates are appointed to posts than men, even successful women feel constrained and frustrated in moving up the career ladder. Only 37% of female respondents expected to reach the higher echelons of their chosen career as opposed to 62% of males. Even in mundane areas, such as dress, 70% of women thought it was important for them to dress well, but only 36% of the same women thought it was important for men to be well-presented. It is perhaps significant that on all the mundane questions only women's opinions were reported.

The statistical information on involvement in professional institutions was not surprising in the light of the above. 43.5% of qualifying barristers are female and yet only 5.9% achieve Q.C. status; 11.8% of Civil Engineering students are female but only 0.1% are fellows of the Institute of Civil Engineering. The 'icing on the cake' for this article in the enlightened 1990s was that 'All respondents agreed that fathers were just as capable of bringing up children but the men thought that it was the mother's job to do it.' Perhaps women accept the child care role because in a male-dominated society there are few credible alternatives, and men will usually avoid child care duties since these do nothing to enhance or maintain their dominant position. This stereotyping role affirmation is ingrained in most societies, so much so that Horner (1968) asked female students to complete a story-line, 'After first-term finals Ann finds herself at the top of her medical school class...'. Male students were given the same story with 'John' as the character – 65% of the female students showed definite signs of avoiding success, whereas with males it was only 10%.

The final beacon of light for gender empowerment comes in the shape of Lesley McDonagh, married with three children, who is mentioned in the article 'First woman among equals' (Appendix 2) by Sharon Wallach. Lesley is the first female managing partner of a City firm. She is pictured as slim, bright and attractive in a typically feminine leggy pose, occupying a suitably warm and softly furnished office. Her rise to this position seems even more amazing given her 'personable and non-aggressive manner, worlds away from a stereotypical City manager.' Lesley does not see herself as ambitious – not for her the imposing desk or stark masculine furniture. Everything suggests that she reached the pinnacle of her career in spite of her femininity. She states that she has never felt the 'glass-ceiling' effect in her career, and that 50% of the firm's fee earners are female. She is also a member of the Law Society, in which eight out of seventy-five members are female. In this unique position she is heralded as a role model for all young women; yet how different the article might have been if the context of her role as career woman had been shifted to the home and her role as mother been highlighted instead. She admits that she works until 7 o'clock at night and that home life begins at 7.15, but with two children under the age of four the extent of that home life must be questionable. According to Lesley her home life runs very smoothly because of 'a good continuation' of nannies; since her husband is also a partner in a City firm presumably he too works unsocial hours. Perhaps the private role has lost out to the demands of the public role – either way women cannot win, for if this article had been written about the first male managing partner then his role as a father would not have been mentioned at all.

Although dictionary definitions are often used to begin essays, this will finish with one. 'To mother' means to nurture and care for; 'to father' is simply to impregnate.

Exercises

In this section we will look at different aspects of the essays you have just been reading:

- Introductions
- Paragraphing
- Use of sources
- Conclusions
- Answering the question

Introductions

1. Compare the introductions to essays 1 and 2. Which of the following is true of which introduction?

    (i) avoids simply re-stating the question
    (ii) establishes a theoretical basis for the answer
    (iii) leads the reader into the main body of the essay
    (iv) distinguishes between different possible approaches to the question
    (v) declares what areas are going to be considered
    (vi) seeks to define relevant concepts

2. Obviously one of these essays has the better introduction! Now look at the beginning of essay 3. How does it compare? (use the list of features given above).

3. If you go back to the beginning of essay 2, you can see that it has a distinct structure based, like all good writing, on a clear division of functions. Those functions might be described, in order, like this (note that the number of functions does not match the number of sentences!):

    (i) introduce definitions of relevant concepts
    (ii) state one possible definition
    (iii) state contrasting definition
    (iv) expand upon preferred definition
    (v) state aims of essay
    (vi) state additional aims of essay (state additional complexity)

Try mapping these functions on to the opening paragraph of essay 2: bracket off the sections that correspond to the functions.

4 Now try to add to and re-write the introduction to essay 3 by using the list of functions listed above.

5 Academic writers should be sparing with words. Make your points crisply and as simply as possible. Re-write the following so that the main points are brought out more economically:

> Most of the power in our country is still controlled by men, you only have to look at the amount of male politicians and members of parliament. Margaret Thatcher became the first female Prime Minister in two thousand years of British History and she became internationally famous because of this. The male Tories were truly overturned, their attitude was that it was so unnatural that a woman's rule should last, they expected Thatcher to have a short ruling, being proved wrong they began to praise her for 'having a mind like a man's', and 'the best man in the Tory party'; she was not praised for being a successful woman, because she had so much power she became 'male'.

Paragraphing

A good introduction, we have seen, makes it clear immediately what different approaches to the question have been grasped. Good paragraphing will show that those aspects are being explored in an orderly and discriminating way.

1. Like introductions, paragraphs have a clear structure, although that structure is likely to be more variable. Look at the third paragraph of essay 2. It obeys the following pattern (map these functions on to the paragraph):

    (i)   topic sentence
    (ii) cite authority (ie Mead) supporting topic sentence
    (iii) give examples cited by authority
    (iv) sum up significance of examples
    (v)   state more complex aspect of that significance
    (vi) conclude: state limitations of (iv) and (v)

Now you try. Write a paragraph about a topic in Sociology you're familiar with, following the list of functions given above.

2. Not all paragraphs will be structured like the one you have just

imitated. In essay 2, turn to paragraphs six ('The family, there-fore...') and eight ('Although appearing to start...'). See if you can describe their different sentence functions.

3. An essay is not just a collection of paragraphs: they all have to fit together. It follows that the topic sentence (see the Summa-ries section in Core Element 5 if you've forgotten what that is) will often stress the relationship of the new paragraph to what has come before – preferably the previous paragraph! Find some topic sentences in any of the three essays which seem, in this light, especially successful or otherwise.

4. Paragraphs have functions, like the sentences they contain. They might:

   (i)   underline an existing point by giving further evidence
   (ii) qualify a point made earlier by citing further evidence
   (iii) explore the consequences of a point already made
   (iv) establish a parallel with a point already made
   (v)   extend the application of a point already made
   (vi) take a completely new direction

Can you find some examples of these paragraph functions in essay 2?

5. In most cases, functions (ii), (iii) and (iv) are the ones most likely to produce a controlled, argumentative essay. Accumulating evidence (i), establishing parallels (iv), and shooting off in a different direction (vi) can be a substitute for real thinking.

When you plan your essay you need to think about the different points you want to make in relation to paragraph functions. Only then can you be confident that you are tackling the question in an orderly way. We will return to this important matter in Answering the Question, below (p.110).

Use of sources

Quoting sources is an essential part of demonstrating that you are on top of your subject. The point is not to blunt your personal awareness of sociological issues, but to sharpen them up by showing that you can use evidence constructively, account for different points of view, and argue against some of them. Remember that you have to record citations properly, as set out in the Referencing section in Core Element 6.

1. Are there any differences between the ways in which sources are used in the three essays you have read?

2. Like paragraphing, source quotation should be dynamic, an occasion for saying something more. Quotations can:
    - (i) add detail to a point already made
    - (ii) show how perceptions of a topic have changed
    - (iii) illustrate disagreements in areas of a topic
    - (iv) demonstrate how partial some research can be

Can you find examples of these in the three essays? Try also to identify moments where the students could have used one of the functions above, but didn't.

3. Can you think of any other constructive things you could do with sources? Look, for example, at what English students and Historians might do (see Use of Sources in the English and History sections of this book).

4. Sociologists weave sources into the fabric of the text. This means that it is not usually a good idea to begin a paragraph by writing 'Noggins (1986) says that...'. The important thing is to let the argument come first, then the evidence for it. Look again at essay 2 and select the items of language which the author used to introduce sources.

5. Now try to improve paragraphs five ('Ferguson') and six ('Research by') of essay 1 by incorporating the sources more effectively, and using one of the paragraph structures identified in the Paragraphing section you have just worked on (p.107).

Conclusions

We've already looked briefly at conclusions in Writing Brief Essays, Core Element 4. Have another look at what you found there and see if you can apply it to the endings of the essays printed here.

1. Which seems to you the most successful conclusion of the three essays, and why?

2. How could any of the three conclusions have been improved?

3. Good conclusions, to make a familiar point, have a structure, just like introductions and paragraphs. Look at the final paragraph of essay 2. The sentences perform the following functions:

(i) topic (affirming relationship of conclusion to the question set)
(ii) conditions underlying topic
(iii) affirm complexity of topic

Needless to say, this is not the only possible way of concluding. It is, nevertheless, a good working model. Use it to tidy up the conclusions to essays 1 and 3.

Answering the question

You've already come to some judgment about how well each of the essays answers the question set. You may have noticed that there are different kinds of question.

1. Look at the following questions and identify the different types:

(a) 'Arguably it is the issue of definition which lies at the heart of the task of understanding poverty.' (Alcock, 1993). Discuss.
(b) Is the concept of social class still useful for understanding aspects of contemporary society?
(c) With the help of examples, explain how Sociology can help us to understand the relationship between 'personal troubles' and 'public issues'.
(d) With reference to the appropriate evidence, examine the suggestion (Health Divide, 1988) that policies to reduce health inequalities would be misguided if they focused entirely on the individual.
(e) To what extent can an understanding of gender issues help to explain social inequalities?
(f) How adequate are explanations of poverty based on the individual?
(g) It has been suggested that 'fundamental self-interest' was a key motive for voting Conservative in the 1992 General Election. Does this mean that the consumer model of voting is more useful in explaining voting behaviour than the class identification model?

2. You've no doubt noticed that Sociology essays are greatly concerned with

(i) evaluating conceptual definitions (eg questions a, b and g in the above list)

(ii) assessing the fit between conceptual definitions and the available evidence (eg questions d and e in the above list)

Whenever a question asks 'How useful...', 'To what extent...', 'How far...', or 'How adequate...' etc, you are required to think about how well the concept you're dealing with fits the range of actual evidence available. What are the implications of this for the way you plan and write an essay?

3. Think about what you've just written in relation to the three essays. The plan for essay 2 might have begun like this, assuming that each point in the list below corresponds to one paragraph in the essay:

---

1. Define social institutions: <u>different</u> definitions – Parsons vs Berger

2. Define gender: historical basis for definition

3. One aspect of gender debate: the question of 'natural' roles. Explore and debate

4. One important institution shaping identity: the family. The family according to different definitions of institutions

---

Now you try to carry on. Reconstruct the plan of paragraphs in brief, from 'Women have a dual role' until the end of the essay:

4. Have you come up against any problems here? How well was the essay planned?

5. You may have found that at every stage of the essay the student has tried to keep in view both the concepts involved and their location in empirical evidence. Are there any moments where a *change* of concept or *refinement* of a concept in use is signalled?

6. Now look at the other essays again. Do they keep in view both the concepts involved and their location in the evidence? Identify moments in each essay where this could have been done more successfully.

Summary: a procedure to follow

So far we've been looking at different aspects of Sociology essays. Now we need to pull everything together in the form of a procedure that you can follow when you write one yourself. Try taking these ten steps:

1. Break down the question (remember the Answering the Question (pp.110–11) section), making sure that you understand it. Where there is a choice of questions, don't go for one immediately without thinking about the others; it might turn out to be more difficult.

2. Research: identify and summarise all the different areas that the question is asking you to consider. Find relevant sources to back up your arguments.

3. Sort out any areas of particular controversy where you can play different sources off against each other.

4. From what you have drawn up so far, decide which of the different areas have priority in your account.

5. Plan: refer back to the Paragraphing section you've just done (p.107–8) and sort out the relationships between the different points you want to make. Make sure that you have enough material for each point to produce a well-constructed paragraph. Remember to show an awareness of the different views which could be taken of the topic. It might be helpful to explain your plan to a friend at this stage – this can be a good way of finding out if it is really logical.

6. Write an introduction which will set out your agenda clearly – check for structure with the Introductions section you have just completed.

7. Get writing: remember to structure each paragraph coherently – check against the Paragraphing section.

8. When you get there, remember to make your conclusion correspond to the pattern suggested in the Conclusions section. Don't add anything new at the last minute.

9. Make sure that you have referenced the essay fully, in accordance with the guidelines set out in Core Element 6.

10. Proofread! Nothing irritates a marker more than careless errors, especially in spelling proper names. (Marx, not Marks! The father of communism was not a clothing retailer!) Try reading the essay out loud to see if it sounds right, and to check that all the full stops, commas, etc are in the right place. Your logical and indulgent friend will appreciate the experience enormously.

Key to Core Element 1

Remember that you are provided with this key just so that you can get going and understand the nature of the exercises. Once you gather momentum, the answers to the other sections will be self-evident.

1. Problem: first paragraph. Solution: second paragraph.

2. Sentences two and three explain the two reasons why there is a problem.

3. The first sentence states the problem and then the number of reasons for it.

4. (ii)

5. 'the sun, which is a typical star'; 'planets do not themselves shine'; 'Even slight differences in a star's light'.

6. made difficult.

7. You need to use a thesaurus!

8. (i).

9. (iii)

10. —

11. High resolution spectroscopy enabled Dr Roger Campbell and his colleagues to get round this problem by allowing them to measure...

12. For example:

    (a) In the past, the search for a way of preventing hereditary diseases was hampered by two factors. Not only was the agent which carried them unknown; even if it had been discovered, there would not have been the technology to assist prevention.

Watson and Crick's discovery in 1953 of the structure of DNA provided the breakthrough. It paved the way for re-combinant technology, which theoretically allowed new genes to be inserted in place of defective ones.

(b) Knowledge of late seventeenth-century social life used to be limited. Random records such as letters, poems, paintings, newspapers and government documents were all the historian had to work with. Much of this material, moreover, came from or related to aristocratic circles. The discovery of Pepys' diary changed all this. Here was a daily record spanning ten years of eating, sleeping, work and sex. Details of houses, servants' behaviour, and other everyday concerns became available as never before.

13. Problem: first paragraph. Solution: second paragraph.

14. (iii)

15. State nature and scale of problem (first sentence); introduce alternatives to one possible solution (third sentence).

16. Emphasises scale of problem.

17. Examples of preferred solutions.

18. (ii)

19. 'be based exclusively on the family model' (this would under-line still further the rigour of the British solution); 'have rapidly developed communities of their own' (many have sprung up in a short space of time) *or* 'their answer to rapidly increasing dependency' (the situation is deteriorating faster than first stated); 'other countries undoubtedly demonstrate' *or* 'there are undoubtedly alternative ways' ('undoubtedly' is often used to underline a point, although it just as often precedes a qualifica-tion: 'it is undoubtedly true that... but the real point is...')

20. (ii)

21. Drop the 'u' from the stem and include it in the tail: humour–humorous; labour–laborious, etc.

22. (i)

23. 'Adopting' suggests something you have come to acquire consciously; 'holding' simply says that you have it.

24. Solution; aspect of solution; re-state problem.

25. —

26. —

27. For example: 'increasing dependency has led elderly people in the United States to develop communities of their own, run for and by themselves'.

28. For example:

> All countries face a crisis in coping with the rising level of crime. It is hard to underestimate the scale of the problem. Not everyone, however, has followed the British example of simply building more prisons.
>
> Japan, for instance, offers state subsidies for jobs in the hope that keeping people in employment will control the incidence of crime. In France, there is massive investment in community facilities designed to foster a sense of social responsibility. Some argue against such expensive options, but they do appear to be effective.
>
> Examples from other countries demonstrate that there are other ways of tackling the issue of crime. Incarceration, with its costly long-term consequences (ex-prisoners re-offend consistently), is not the only solution.

Key to Core Element 2

1. (a) ...Malcolm hesitated to...

   (b) ...Brian... went straight to...

   (c) ...Joe always carried a small motor-bike...

   (d) Denise... hit the target...

   (e) Fiona... was... one of the best climbers...

2. For example:

   (a) Malcolm's friends urged him to join them in their plan to glide off Ben Ormond at midnight, but, much as he liked hang-gliding, he hesitated because he considered it too dangerous.

   (b) The eccentric ironmonger in Bromyard sometimes forgot to open his shop, to the disappointment of Brian, who always went straight there in search of bargains whenever he visited the town.

   (c) Bandits living in the mountains preyed on travellers, especially those who were forced to spend the night there, so Joe always carried a small motor-bike in the back of his van to use as a means of rapid escape from the threat of such an attack if he should break down on the twisting mountain roads.

   (d) The students in the class usually missed the target even after many hours' practice, much to the frustration of the instructor, who was doing his best to coach them; whereas Denise, who had been coached by her elder brother, the European champion, hit the target again and again.

   (e) Fiona's instructors agreed that she was one of the best divers they had ever had the pleasure of training, even though she had never even been in a boat before coming on the course and, moreover, suffered from acute asthma.

3. For example:

   (a) The wall was extremely large, so in order to paint it the decorators used a special roller which enabled them to cover the most distant corners. (In the original version the word 'so' repeats the sense of 'In order to'.)

   (b) This is perfectly acceptable, whatever you may think of the content.

   (c) When he first bought the house he didn't like the way it was decorated, so, in spite of the time and expense involved, he re-decorated it to his own taste. (In the original version there is no main clause).

   (d) They ran to a large tree in the corner of the field, which sheltered them until the storm abated. (The original version needs a relative clause to show how each part of the [non] sentence is related to the others.)

   (e) We want our customers to be satisfied, so if you have a complaint write to the address below, saying where you purchased the goods and when. (The original is nonsense, since it implies that the firm only wants its customers to be satisfied if they have a complaint.)

   (f) The Queen, who was wearing a cherry coat with matching hat and ear-rings, was accompanied to the aeroplane by the Duke. (NB In the original version it is the Duke who is wearing the coat, hat and ear-rings!)

Also available from Kogan Page